REACHING YOUNG ADULTS:
EQUIPPING, EMPOWERING, AND ENERGIZING YOUR CHURCH FOR THE FUTURE

DR. RICHARD C. FLIPPIN

FLIPPIN LEGACY MINISTRIES
Raising Leaders Around The World

CONTENTS

FOREWARD

Isn't it interesting that as we get older there are diminishing voices in our lives? When we were children, we had parents and other adult voices directing, guiding, counseling, correcting and instructing us. Then, when we get of a certain age, there seems to be this mutual disengagement in which we have fewer or no voices acting as guardrails for life.

This disconnect is evidenced in the life, structure and programming of a church. Children's ministries feed the youth ministry that feed young adult ministry etc. Well, that's how it should be theoretically. But you would agree that while much intentional time, energy, finances, facilities, programming, and staffing is focused on children and youth but slides off the radar for young adults.

Just when young adults need more engagement, at all levels, they start disengaging because most churches have no strategy to escalate engagement with young adults. Young adults, as a general demographic, bring vibrancy, innovation, creativity, energy, relationships—they are the sustainability plan for a church.

A church grows older with the Senior Pastor. That is a fact. Therefore it takes very high levels of intentionality to focus on transgenerational sustainability. Young adults spawn families and bring their children to church reaching even deeper into the pool of the church.

It is with this burden that Dr. Richard C. Flippin writes REACHING YOUNG ADULTS IN YOUR CHURCH: EQUIPPING, EMPOWERING AND ENERGIZING YOUR CHURCH FOR THE FUTURE.

The Bible is replete with "young adults" who challenged and changed their worlds—Joseph, Daniel, Esther—Jesus! The Scriptures inform us that Jesus was about thirty years of age when he began his ministry.

Every church can continue and enhance its vibrant life-giving future by REACHING YOUNG ADULTS IN YOUR CHURCH: EQUIPPING, EMPOWERING AND ENERGIZING YOUR CHURCH FOR THE FUTURE.

-Dr. Samuel R. Chand

<u>DEDICATION</u>

This Book is Dedicated to:

The memory of Richard and Virginia Flippin and Rev. Moses and Earline Taylor, Sr. whose spirit and blood continues to run through my veins; whose shoulders I stand upon as a great patron of their life works, innumerable sacrifice and dedication towards my brothers, sister, cousins, and the host of generations that will come long after us. I am grateful now they are among the host of my ancestors who are that great cloud of witnesses cheering me on.

and to

The present and future preachers of the gospel; My colleagues in the ministry who are often misunderstood as a spokesperson of God, criticized as a servant of the people and who are never given the proper recognition for their endless sacrifice, devotion, and contribution towards the ministry. It is my sincere prayer that each word strengthens your calling the more, ignite your spirit further, and reinforce your zest greater to continue to seek the lost, guide the misplaced, and preach a resounding gospel to the forgotten as we help someone as we pass along so our living will not be in vain. We do this to HIS Glory.

<u>ACKNOWLEGEMENT</u>

Thank you is the best prayer that anyone could say.

-Alice Walker

For the past twenty-five years, I am indeed blessed and grateful to have grown-up in a loving and nurturing church that always encourages and prays for me in both my present and future endeavors. Thereby, it is a tremendous task to reflect and acknowledge all those who have supported my aspirations, encouraged my endeavors and prayed for my resilience during a rewarding progression. It is difficult to pen all the names that assisted me with completing my first published book because so many have committed and sacrificed along with me to make this published work successful. Therefore, I want to acknowledge those who closely worked with me; for their time I am most appreciative.

First, I want to thank **Rev. Dr. Jeffrey Haggray** for his guidance and availability; I am further appreciative for him always being available and assisting me with properly structuring and assuring the contexts within the book is applicable. Next, I am thankful to **Ms. Keiya Grady** and **Ms. JuJuan Grady** for their extensive research on my behalf and assisting me with developing and articulating soundly my theological component to reflect my application. Thusly, I am especially thankful, **Ms. Crystal Choates,** for her many countless reviews, revisions and edits on my behalf. Throughout the process, she challenged my thinking, my approaches, and my writing to make the contexts within my research even stronger. I am again appreciative for her service and being with me along this journey. I am also indebted to **Dr. Jamie**

Wilson, Jr., *Mrs. Teresa McKenzie, and Ms. Ola Kakolesha* for their many revisions, insights and suggestion of making this a conventional book. I am appreciative to my Morehouse College, my fraternity and confidant in ministry, *Pastor Wendel Dandridge* for formatting the final work and his many suggestions during my writing and editing phase.

To *Mr. and Mrs. Edgar and Clarice Derricho*, who allowed me for several months to research and shadow them; who answered all my questions towards their leadership process and who permitted me to chronicle their odyssey as prospective leaders of my (The Greater Piney Grove Baptist) church to now servant leaders. I am thankful they consented me to witness their transformation as servant leaders. Lastly, I want to thank, my Senior Pastor, *Dr. William E. Flippin, Sr.,* who is a strong model leader of his own, who allowed me permission for this research to take place; and my much-loved church family, *The Greater Piney Grove Baptist Church* for allowing me to chronicle our rich history as we celebrated in our yearlong centennial anniversary in 2014, when this research was being authored, our past achievements, commemorated our present triumphs and as now we continue to rejoice in our future promises.

THE PURPOSE OF THE BOOK

In my extensive research, as a result of a sharp shift of membership in active young adults between 18 and 39 years of age in many African American churches, I decided to develop and implement an effective leadership model that will attract, **equip**, **empower** and **energize** young adults, ages 18-39, to assume leadership roles within a reasonable timeframe.

The purpose of the book is to ensure survival of the African American church to a modern-day church by embracing new, vibrant, and relevant leadership structures that focuses on 18-39 years of age to reflect a multi-generation, without the compromise of the church's traditional and religious dynamics.

INTRODUCTION

"A leader lives with people to know their problems. A leader lives with God in order to solve them."[1]

-John C. Maxwell

As I reflect on the progression of the journey of my ministry, I am often reminded of a quote from Reverend Dr. John Maxwell in many of his leadership seminars and books. He states there are two important days in one's life; *one is the day a person is born and the other is the day a person discovers the purpose of why they are born.* Like so many past and present leaders, often I pose this same question of why I was born, especially in my ministry quests.

Interestingly, all my life I have been fascinated with the role of leadership in the likes of the civil rights drum major, Dr. Martin Luther King, Jr., the great emancipator, Abraham Lincoln, the political trailblazer, Hillary Clinton, and currently, our country's first African American President, President Barak Obama, to name a few. In observing their leadership characteristics, I frequently speculate as to what makes a leader noble or undesirable. One enduring question I would ask is, how are the aforementioned leaders and any other leaders able to write their success stories while remaining strong despite vulnerabilities, life challenges, and difficult defeats. Finally, I contemplated whether leaders come to the pivotal point in their lives like me where they have to ask themselves what is the true significance of their lives?

---

[1] John C. Maxwell, *The 21 Irrefutable Laws of Leadership*, (Nashville: Thomas Nelson, 1998), 11-12.

The process of my seeking to discover the purpose of my birth and life began as a young boy growing up in the household of a minister. I always had an affinity towards and a great admiration for ministers; especially given my father and late grandfather were a part of the profession. Being raised in a family of ministers, I was exposed to the importance and sacredness of the call to ministry. I have a strong passion for the great joy of assisting God's people, sacrifice of ministry, and the responsibility of serving the greater community. As a result of my upbringing, I knew serving God's people, and the greater community, would always have a direct connection to the purpose of my birth and thus my life. Early on, I always knew I would find myself in a career of service. Most young children stake claims on what their desired occupation would be in life unfortunately I was undecided. Growing up, I was certain I had no desire to follow the generational path of a minister like my father and grandfather due to the countless responsibilities and obligation of ministry I witnessed. Consequently, through my high school and college years I ignored the call to ministry, and refused to follow in my father and grandfather's ministry footsteps. I decided to pursue a career in education like my mother as it satisfied my yearning and desire to serve God's people.

It was not until my college years at Morehouse College that I began to feel the initial sensation of the purpose of my birth, thus my life. While at Morehouse College, similar to Morehouse Alum, Martin Luther King, Jr., I too felt the great sense to serve. However during this time, I questioned how would I serve? Like young Martin Luther King, Jr. during his college years, I too embarked on the decisive question of, how *I* serve and more importantly how would I leave a lasting impression on my community, and future generations through the rendering of my service? Initially, I thought I would serve, similar to how my mother served as an educator, through the metro Atlanta school system. As an educator, I could serve my community by becoming a mentor and a big brother figure for young men and women to as they each aspire to be effective leaders in their respective community. I answered the call to ministry in my junior year at Morehouse College just as Martin Luther King Jr. did. I too would describe my calling towards ministry as, an inner urge calling me to serve humanity.[2] Therefore, during this time, similar to so many leaders and preachers alike, I could no longer ignore my call and responsibility towards ministry and more importantly, to the greater community. However, over time, I realized my urgency to serve was not through the school system, but in ministry, a vocation similar to my late grandfather and father. As I continued to determine the reason I was born, and when I made the decision to enter professional ministry in 2004, I assumed I would immediately make an instant lasting impact and enhance the church's life, its structure and its congregants for the greater, more so than any of my minister predecessors. I was under the false impression that I was the Church's answer to all of its previous issues. I was the only conundrum solver. I soon realized I was mistaken as I began to establish my destiny in ministry. In my naïve state, I thought the reason why I was born was to smile like a politician, kiss babies for photo opportunities, comfort the bereaved in time of

---

[2] King, Jr., Martin Luther, Clayborne Carson (Editor), Ralph E. Luker (Editor) and Denny A. Russell (Editor), *The Papers of Martin Luther King, Jr.: Volume 1: Called to Serve, January, 1929-June, 1951.* (Martin Luther King Papers) [Hardcopy]. California: University of California, 1992, 363.

sorrow, and preach until the kingdom of heaven descended on Earth each glorious Sunday morning. Consequently, because of my preconceived notion of ministry and the meaning of why I was born, I fully expected to be the unparalleled paradigm leader whom everyone wanted to hear when preached to; seek guidance when lost, come to for answers to life's unconcealed questions, and wanted to follow into the new Promised Land of new expectations; I sought to be the prototype preacher. More so, I thought I would have no opposition, no setbacks, and become the first leader to go unchallenged in my ministry profession.

Nevertheless, my narrow awareness of the ministry expanded on biblical principles that would shed light on my desire to discover the reason I existed through the passage of scripture when Jesus taught his disciples a noteworthy lesson on being the greatest. In other words, Jesus instructs his disciples who wrongly associated greatness with power, position and prestige. In the disciple's aspiration to be like Christ, they were using the wrong avenues, such as a heavenly position, like sitting on the right and left hand of Christ to secure a place in heaven instead of the true essence of being a servant leader. Jesus, particularly in Matthew 23:11, explains to his followers to be great, to become the greatest, in the sight of God, one must learn the temperament of service not through position, power and prestige but through the simple act of service.[3] Jesus emphasized to the disciples that to be the greatest, one must become a servant to all. Similarly, peaceful, non-violent prolific leader, Mahatma Gandhi took Jesus' concept of being great through the performance of a servant deposition

---

[3] Matthew 23:11 (King James Version)

4

further when he emphasizes, *The best way to find yourself is to lose yourself in the service of others.*[4] Ultimately, I found that my destiny and purpose divinely ordered for me to be a servant to all and to lose myself in serving others. I desire to be a servant leader in such a way that I will be able to equip, empower, and energize others to be effective leaders both within the church and in the greater community.

Currently, I serve as the Executive Pastor of The Greater Piney Grove Baptist Church, Atlanta, GA, where my father, Rev. Dr. William E. Flippin, Sr., serves as the Senior Pastor. The Greater Piney Grove Baptist Church's current demographic is approximately 2,500 active family African American Baptist Church in the metro Atlanta area with a long history of community service and outreach. During the calendar year of 2014, my church will have a centennial anniversary celebration as we observe one hundred years of past achievements, commemorate present triumphs, and rejoice in our future promises. Additionally this year, we will complete the building of our new 1,500-seat worship center that will also house a state-of-the art community outreach center.

One of the many roles as Executive Pastor is to serve as the Director of Organization Ministry Planning and Projects. In this position, my task is to promote interconnected fellowship activities to the congregation for the purpose of building unity in the body of Christ through small groups such as Sunday School Classes, weekly Bible Study, and ministry meetings to name a few. Secondly, my responsibility is to serve as a liaison between the Senior Pastor and all ministry leaders to

---

[4] Mahatma Gandhi, Brainy Quotes, *Servanthood,*
http://www.brainyquote.com/quotes/quotes/m/mahatmagan150725.html
(accessed March 13, 2014).

ensure constant communication and open dialogue between the Senior Pastor, the Senior Leadership and our members. Lastly, my responsibility to the congregants is to encourage spiritual growth, love and connect them with others through biblical principles, ministry opportunities, mission and prayer.

In my tenure at The Greater Piney Grove Baptist Church, affectionately known in the community as "The Grove," I have observed various seasons in our rich and vibrant history; seasons of celebration, uncertainty, challenges, setbacks, and triumphs. Consequently, my position stemmed from a time in our church history when it was showing a decline in it membership. Within the past five years, our church membership has resulted from 4,000 active members to its present 2,500 active families. Why has our membership decreased in the past five years? Presently, the majority of the church's decision-making body and the Senior leadership team are comprised mostly of leaders age 55 and above.

The majority age demographic of church membership range from 20-45. Therefore, the disproportion transpiring within the church is that the senior leadership, which makes imperative and out-dated decisions, does not reflect the current status of a more contemporary, pristine church demographic. Consequently, the church is in a decline of obliteration rather than an incline of relevancy. Secondly, the apprehension between the senior leadership team and a diverse church membership is in the senior leadership's assessment. The senior leadership's judgments are conservative, irrelevant and unbeneficial to the future outlook of the church. In addition, the senior leadership is praising our church's past achievements while being blinded to our church's future expectations. Whereas the current diverse membership are more innovative, futuristic thinkers, driven by technology and more-so risk takers for the advancement of the church. Thereby, in my preliminary analysis of the fate of my church, if my church is going to survive in the 21st century and still be relevant and progressive, the church leadership has to train more leaders within the age bracket of 20-45, so it can always mirror the demographic of its church membership. The senior leadership team's age range presents an imbalance relative to the needs and wants of the diverse membership, causing a huge disconnect. This approach to decision-making, and lack of representation of the diverse membership, has resulted in young adults ages 18-39 within the church becoming discontented and unmotivated to invest in the church's future or train to become a leader.

As a result of this disconnect, the lack of motivation and state of being discontented, the question is, what kind of a leadership program will empower young adults (18-39) to assume leadership roles within a faster timeframe at a traditional, Baptist church in Atlanta, Georgia? As I approach this question, I recognize there will be great challenges for me as I set out a course to develop leaders from the ages 18-39 in a church that is built on traditional, senior leadership. Therefore, the question arises, "How do I equip, empower, and energize young adults who attend The Greater Piney Grove Baptist Church to be faithful through traditional dynamics?"

I desire to be a servant leader among those who are ready to take charge and improve the life and spirit of The Greater Piney Grove

Baptist Church. In this transition phase of our church, I know there will be many challenges, obstacles, tension, and questions about the process we are embarking on with the passing of the mantle. However, to be a successful church and to establish new growth, we embrace new ideas, approaches through shared power, yet not neglect our tradition that brought us to this point.

The purpose of this undertaking is to give the reader a glimpse of the history, social climate, and present reality of The Greater Piney Grove Baptist Church. As a result of our current disposition, it is my desire to develop a twelve-month comprehensive leadership program and a paradigm to follow that will empower young adults to assume leadership roles within a faster timeframe than the current schedule. This will be accomplished by a twelve month comprehensive leadership training program with biblical principles of leadership. This program will be knowledge driven to include a systematic approach to bible study, and a mentorship program that is driven by the results of this case study that addresses the social climate of this environment.

I will attempt to answer the question, What kind of a leadership program will empower young adults to assume leadership roles within a faster timeframe at a traditional, Baptist church in Atlanta, Georgia by highlighting in the first chapter, the history, and cultural dynamics of The Greater Piney Grove Baptist Church, and the reason our decision making team consists of members who are over the age of 55. Next, in the theological chapter, I will justify the 21st century Baptist church model of leadership through relationship, spiritual covenant, and mentorship. Thus, this will enable me to develop a course to attract potential leaders, young adults, to be equipped, empowered, and energized to strengthen our church without compromising our heritage and history. Finally, all these practices will allow The Greater Piney Baptist Church, and me to pose the question, 'where do we go from here by building unity amidst diversity as servant leaders.

In order to correct this problem of a declining church, I feel our church must develop new leaders within our church by equipping, empowering, and energizing each with the traditional values of our church while transforming new leaders and our church for the betterment of the 21st century.

Browse the business section of any bookstore, read any magazines, thumb through any articles and you'll discover countless books on leadership.

We can load ourselves up with leadership lessons from famous coaches, generals and successful businesspeople. We have our pick in Vince Lombardi, General Colin Powell, Phil Jackson, the mogul empire of Beyonce', Jay-Z and from the first African American President, President Barack Obama and many more.

If we want a more classical leadership style, there are also books that extract beneficial leadership concepts from the lives of the great men of history. From the leadership style, struggle and approach of Lincoln, Martin Luther King, Jr., Kennedy, Churchill and many others.

As I researched, read on this subject matter of keen leadership, I have been encouraged, the more, uplifted, challenge and rewarded as a result. However, learning leadership from a Christian perspective

9

requires a very different approach. To successful gasp leadership from a Christian vantage point, one must identify a Christian leader. Someone of whom we can model ourselves after without a doubt, the greatest demonstration of Christian leadership is the example of Jesus Christ.

In any type of leadership style, it is simple not enough to imitate anyone, in this case Jesus, to act out the pattern of leadership revealed throughout Jesus' life. Regardless of how devoted and diligent we must be we will always fall short of his many examples. I am convinced, as sure I am sure many are, of the worthiness of his goal and one need to follow the leadership model of Jesus, the Christ.[5]

---

[5] Gerald Brooks, Jesus on Leadership, (Plano: Gerald Brooks, 2007), 1-2.

Chapter 1

"Know from whence you came. If you know whence you came, there are absolutely no limitations to where you can go."[6]

-James Baldwin

The Greater Piney Grove Baptist Church has a long, rich history that stems from its humble beginnings in Atlanta's Historic Old Fourth Ward in 1914 to its present location in Southeast Atlanta at 1879-1921 Glenwood Avenue. As of its centennial year, The Greater Piney Grove Baptist Church has called only five pastors. Each pastor has left a lasting impression. Pastors have made the church stronger in its witness and more secure after their respective departure. Furthermore, each pastor brought a sense of community involvement, outreach emphasis, spiritual renewal, and development. In 2014, The Greater Piney Grove Baptist Church family celebrates its yearlong centennial anniversary and we climax the year with the erection of a new fifteen-hundred-seat sanctuary. Since August of 2007, I have served as the Executive Pastor of The Greater Piney Grove Baptist Church in Atlanta, Georgia. To serve along with my father, Dr. William E. Flippin, Sr., who has been the Senior Pastor since 1990, is a great honor.

The Greater Piney Grove Baptist Church, affectionately known as "The Grove" or "Piney Grove" in the metro Atlanta community now has approximately 2,500 families of which are African-American families.

---

[6] James Baldwin, Goodreads- Quotable Quote, *Knowing*
http://www.goodreads.com/quotes/14373-know-from-whence-you-came-if-you-know-whence-you. (accessed March 13, 2014).

The church's motto is "The Church with Helping Hands." Once a person enters one of the three Sunday morning worship services and leaves the church campus, one cannot help but feel the warm spirit of the congregation and embrace how the church indeed loves God and enjoys serving God's people.

A fundamental question will begin our historical quest, "How did Piney Grove Baptist Church get from 101 Bell Street to 101 Boulevard and now to its current site at 1879 Glenwood Avenue?" The history of Piney Grove is unique, rich, and inspirational.

Piney Grove's history is distinctive in that it is a predominately African American Church founded in the state of Georgia during the Jim Crow Era. At the opening of the twentieth century, the United States was plagued with many economic and social issues, and African Americans found themselves attempting to cope and simply survive. Piney Grove's history was further distinguished by being situated in the heart of the Old Fourth Ward, a Black community cultivated by its surroundings. During this era, racial tension was very prevalent. During this era, Atlanta was an urban city with laws on segregation ordinances that designated blocks based on race.

An essential formula for African American's survival was to maintain a separate existence socially and culturally. An important agency for maintaining group cohesion and rendering self-help was the church. The birth of The Grove is compelling and inspirational because Piney Grove Baptist Church, as it was first named, was established as a gathering of Christian souls who felt the need to organize a church for the continued nourishment of the Lord's word and for the edification of God's people.

In 1914, the Rev. N. J. Jenkins founded and organized the church in a three-room house located at 101 Bell Street in the northeast Atlanta. The selection of the name "Piney Grove" is still a mystery even today; however, the small band of worshipers first met on the 2nd and 4th Sunday of each month. Its distinct, initial location was along side several major streets and intersections and newly formed black churches. The founding home of Piney Grove was nestled along side great historical black churches such as Wheat Street Baptist Church, Big Bethel A.M.E and Ebenezer Baptist Church. Ebenezer Baptist Church is where the legendary Civil Rights Leader, Rev. Martin Luther King, Jr., served as Co-Pastor. Interestingly, the congregational composition of Wheat Street, Big Bethel, and Ebenezer Baptist Churches was of the educated elite families. Piney Grove catered more to the underprivileged, working class. As a result, the church was known in the community, during this time, as a church that met the needs of a distressed area. Piney Grove was walking on its path of destiny by embodying the present day motto of, *The Church With Helping Hands,* nearly 80 years before it was established.

Just two years into his pastorate, Rev. N. J. Jenkins resigned as the first pastor of Piney Grove due to his failing health. However, in his legacy, he planted a seed, which over the course of the next eight decades would flourish into a phenomenal institution of worship and social change, and have a profound impact on the community. In a sense, Rev. Jenkins' leadership established Piney Grove as an organized agent of change that entered the decade of the "Roaring Twenties" committed to do God's will.

In 1916, Rev. Jenkins appointed the second pastor of Piney Grove, the Rev. James D. Sims. As the newly appointed pastor of the Piney Grove congregation, Rev. J. D. Sims continued the role of a vital leader both in the church and within the community. While still in its infancy, in 1917, just three years after it's founding, Piney Grove suffered one of the worst devastations the city had ever seen, the Great Fire of Atlanta. Thousands of Fourth Ward residents' homes and personal property were destroyed, including some members of this newly established church. Early on, Piney Grove had a strong sense of community outreach as it joined with other churches within communities in helping to aid those dislocated by the fire and reiterating the church's present motto.

After almost twenty-five years, in 1939, Piney Grove moved from 101 Bell Street to 101 Boulevard Avenue. This move provided a larger facility, more stability among the congregation, and better resources to aid the membership and the surrounding community. Rev. Sims served faithfully from 1916 to 1941. The third pastor called was Rev. A. R. Barnette. Reverend Barnette served the congregation from 1941 to 1955.

In the church's records, minimum deeds are written about Rev. Barnette's accomplishments as pastor; however, his legacy sustained the church during a critical period in American history. He stabilized the church's well-being and tradition during the aftermath of the Great Depression, the impact of World War II, and the impending Civil

14

Rights Movement. He helped define Piney Grove as a church capable of standing during challenging economic times, war, and social changes.

After Rev. A. R. Barnette, the church called its fourth pastor, Rev. Frank Jones. Rev. Jones has been the longest serving pastor of Piney Grove and the most celebrated pastor in its history. Rev. Jones led the Piney Grove congregation from 1956 until his passing in September 1989, reminiscent of how Moses led the Israelites. The legacy of Rev. Frank Jones is embedded in his insight to modify the name of Piney Grove Baptist Church to what it is currently known as, The Greater Piney Grove Baptist Church. The purpose of the name modification was to envision the church to become greater in all aspects of ministry and community service.

Moreover, the leadership of Rev. Frank Jones was distinguished because in 1971 he took a noble risk by moving the church from the comfort and refuge of 101 Boulevard, the established black community, to the discomfort and unpleasant suburb where the present edifice stands at 1879 Glenwood Avenue. The relocation of Greater Piney Grove can be compared to the Exodus of the Israelites from Egypt.

As history tells the story, Rev. Jones' leadership and decision to embark upon this great migration was met with boundless resistance, vast opposition, and more importantly, faint questions. However, Rev. Frank Jones sensed if the church was ever going to be known as "greater" in the community and in its future history, it had to take a risk to leave the comfort and safe pasture of 101 Boulevard and cross over to the unfamiliar grounds of 1879 Glenwood Avenue. It was

15

evident his vision was permeated with the spirit of God. The Greater Piney Grove Baptist Church family continues to reap the many benefits of this gallant move and the visionary pastor.

Ultimately, the foresight of Rev. Frank Jones made him a profound, dedicated community leader, preacher, teacher, and administrator. He was a pastor that was dearly loved by his church, and the surrounding community. He was one who was indeed ahead of his time, yet his pastorate dictates that he knew clearly the promising prospect of The Greater Piney Grove Baptist Church.

After the loss of Rev. Frank Jones, the church called its fifth and current pastor, the Rev. Dr. William E. Flippin, Sr., in September 1990. The death of Rev. Frank Jones, and the call of Rev. William Flippin, can be compared to the death of Moses and the call of Joshua. *After the death of Moses the servant of the LORD, the LORD said to Joshua son of Nun, Moses' aide: "Moses my servant is dead. Now then, you and all these people, get ready to cross the Jordan River into the land I am about to give to them—to the Israelites. I will give you every place where you set your foot, as I promised Moses[7].* Likewise, in the passing of the mantle from Rev. Jones to Rev. Flippin, God promised The Greater Piney Grove Baptist Church congregation that the legacy of not only Rev. Jones, but also Reverends, N. J. Jenkins, James D. Sims, and A. R. Barnette would be fulfilled; and the church would continue to be prosperous and become a spiritual beacon to so many, still well beyond the twenty-first century.

---

[7] Joshua 1:1-3 (New International Version).

16

Rev. Flippin Sr., like his predecessors, continues to have a strong and essential presence in the church and community alike. His leadership and pastoral approach stresses community involvement, outreach growth, and holistic rejuvenation.

In 1996, the rapid growth and expansion of the church membership under the leadership of Rev. William E. Flippin Sr. prompted the church to build a multipurpose Family Life Center. The facility houses a gymnasium, child development center, bookstore, library, conference room, and classrooms that better serve the church and the surrounding community. Also, during this year, Rev. William E. Flippin Sr. and the church purchased over thirty acres of land for a new church edifice and for ministry expansion. The church regarded these thirty acres as the "Promised Land."

Similar to the story of Moses and the children of Israel, The Greater Piney Grove Baptist Church too was tested and endured a "wilderness experience" shortly after it purchased and secured its "promised land." For many years, the "promised land" idea was met with uninvited hostility, unfavorable resistance, and unforeseen struggles. During this "wilderness experience," the pastor, many of the leaders, and the parishioners all doubted God and questioned themselves in conquering it's "promised land" and if God's assurance indeed would be fulfilled.

Now then, you and all these people, get ready to cross the Jordan River into the land I am about to give to them—to the Israelites. I will give you every place where you set your foot, as I promised Moses.[8] Sixteen years after the purchase of the "Promised Land" the legacy of

---

[8] Joshua 1:2-4 (New International Version).

Reverends Jenkins, Sims, Barnette, Jones, and the vision of Rev. William E. Flippin Sr. is being fulfilled. On the summer afternoon of August 11, 2012, The Greater Piney Grove Baptist Church held a ground breaking ceremony on its "promised land" which will house a Senior Community Housing Complex and a fifteen-hundred seat sanctuary on its thirty acre church campus.

The Greater Piney Grove Baptist Church is tremendously blessed, in its one hundred years of existence, to have five successfully prominent pastors in both the church and community. Each pastor made the church more distinguished, affluent and renowned. History has proven again, the church's membership is secure and follows good leadership. The Greater Piney Grove Baptist Church is a church that lives out its motto each day as the "Church with Helping Hands," and wants all those who enter to leave out better than they came in.

THE CULTURE DYNAMICS OF THE GREATER PINEY GROVE CHURCH

The Re-Establishment of a Declining Church

CULTURE DYNAMIC DIFFERENCES: THE SUCCESS OF CHIPOTLE

McDonald's deserves a lot of credit for spotting Chipotle when it was just a local Denver chain. And even more credit for betting millions on its potential. However, years later, McDonald's could use a little of that Chipotle magic once again.

Initially when Chipotle first opened, it spent eight years taking McDonald's money, all the while resisting changes to McDonald's reproduction of "fast casual" dining model. With funding from the industry legend McDonald, Chipotle opened hundreds of new stores and built a business that threatens its former partner's market position because of McDonald's conservative apprehensions.

The dissimilar cultural contrast occurred between the traditional tyrants of McDonald's method of stale drive-through menus and Chipotle vision of a more progressive-innovative prototype of fast food operation system that provides better quality, premium food selections with a formal restaurant ambiance. Chipotle executives attribute much of their success to doing things totally differently than McDonald's model, and ignoring McDonald's out-dated manual of fast food by providing consumers the freedom to make their own meals with variety of choices to decide upon.

And because McDonald's ignored change, unwelcome future

expansion, and disregarded potential development, in the beginning of 2015, McDonald's reported awful earnings and warned that the first half of 2015 will be a challenge. [9] Consequently, due to greeting change, being receptive to innovative growth, Chipotle is now flourishing, thriving and trendsetters for the new standard of how to operate restaurants in 2015.

The downfall of McDonald's, like so many churches, McDonald's was not willing to change its method, modify its model and more importantly transform its vision for future growth because they were content with settling for the same. As a result of being comfortable with remaining the same, they lost their focus which made them a successful food chain, their drive and their vision for future expansion. If a person wants growth, they have to ultimately embrace change by doing something they've never done before, to get somewhere they've never been before. Consequently, many churches today are non-existence, and lack futuristic vision because they are uncomfortable to change; more importantly to change for enhancement and continued development. However, if a church and its leader ever want to change, they have to be willing at times to get uncomfortable. So, the question is in leadership expansion and church development, *Are you willing to get uncomfortable?*

In serving as Executive Pastor at The Greater Piney Grove Baptist Church, I can attest to the unease of change in the cultural dynamics that has taken place under the current leadership of its Senior Pastor, Rev. William E. Flippin, Sr. who has served and lead the congregation

---

[9] *http://money.cnn.com/2015/02/03/news/companies/mcdonalds-chipotle/index.html* 20

for over twenty years. When the Senior Pastor was inaugurated as leader, the church was in a shifting phase as it relates to cultural dynamics, given the absence of a formal leader for over a year. Rev. William E. Flippin, Sr. appropriated time to turn the church around by establishing a smoother cultural climate and mindset within the body of Christians at The Greater Piney Grove Baptist Church. The new leadership has worked steadily to take this regressive church into our present season of harvest. As a result, progressive expansions of the congregation and the multiple serving ministries have flourished tremendously. Over twenty years of membership in this church and serving on the ministerial staff and leadership team, I can confidently say that long strides of restructuring our goals as a church has helped lead to a re-established church that is sustainable and progressive.

Prior to the current Senior Pastor, the congregation of The Greater Piney Grove Baptist Church relocated its physical location from the urban inner city to a middle class community, but not its social culture. However, after this massive cultural shift and transition, this in turn, led to the church suffering great loss and division. Although the members of the congregation did the best they could to maintain the rituals and routines of service and worship, the church began to plummet in this community that was very different from the community from whence they came.

In contrast to The Greater Piney Grove today, the declining church before our Senior Pastor's arrival was in total disarray. Before plummeting into the declining phase, The Greater Piney Grove had been prominent. It once flourished in the community with the existence of well servicing sub-cultures within the church. The deacons, trustees, and choir ministries were a major and influential dynamic during this period. However, the death of the pastor, Reverend Frank Jones in 1989 left the church staggering and ultimately ending up in the declining phase of the church's lifecycle.

In 1990, The Greater Piney Grove Baptist Church found itself in the declining slope phase. The great decline was largely due to the church operating without a Pastor or formal leader. In the absence of consistent leadership, the vision and mission of the church were under a thick cloud of fog. Things at the church quickly fell apart. Following the church's one year void of leadership, a new Senior Pastor came abroad. In 1990, the church consisted of a small membership population of working-class citizens, who suffered the effect of not having a pastor, successor or succession plan. The faithful, however remained strong and held the church together. However the membership and its leadership still kept the desire to hold the church together without a primary leader. Likewise, in 2007, this same fate of a declining church met us with the question about our future and community in part. In 2007 becoming a leader during this time was a very arduous undertaking. However, with a new administration team, distinct vision, vibrant ideas, and clear goals, I firmly believed things would shift to a better state.

Consequently, with the church displaying distinct signs of decline, the Senior Pastor and the newly formed leadership team had to quickly undergo a massive model of transformation. In modeling and observing the Senior Pastor, I noticed how he was able to sit with his newly appointed leadership & administration team to outline the issues and needs of the declining degenerate church to become a thriving and healthy church. The transformation cycle would take close to twenty years for complete transition, culture shift and reestablishment. The revised leadership structure consists of, the Senior Pastor, the Executive Pastor, Co-Chairman of Servant Leadership, Chairman of the Board of Trustees, the Chief Administrator and two laity.

One of the important dynamics the newly appointed leadership team faced was its age demographic, which was comprised of leaders fifty-five years of age and older. While the current leadership team has made great strides with representing the demographic of the church body, there is more work to be done to refine this process. In turn, the leadership team conducted a needs assessment in an effort to make clear the areas that needed immediate and extra support, alongside transformation and new initiatives.

In careful study of the church dynamics, recurring threads of observation revealed some very important data and feedback. As a result, some barriers confronted the new leadership as it relates to culture. The first observation was that the majority of the church members were older, conservative, and upheld tradition to governing the church. These members were very comfortable with church being the same as it had been since the beginning of its establishment. Our new leadership was able to note rather quickly, that there was not only a divide in age but also a lack in mission and vision.

Another observation was the present membership demographic did not reflect or mirror the elements and diversity of the surrounding middle class, young adult, African American family and community. This layer also related to the lack of youth that were attending and involved in church. Lastly, the study revealed a lack of modern day equipment and effective resources that seemed to lend to the hindrance in moving this church from a declining phase, surpassing the dynamic phase that had all led us to the re-established phase.

Alongside the new leadership and administration, I worked closely with the new administration team in the development of a roadmap for preparing our church to regain membership and to blossom in worship and serving in its efforts to re-emerge with a new leadership paradigm. For most of the congregation a more progressive administration and leadership was totally new for the, traditional and modern-conservative members.

After careful analysis of the cultural dynamics of this church, the first initiative of our new leadership was to drive the church's rebirth with a sound mission and vision. It was necessary to have a roadmap that was clearly designed to move the church forward. The church's preceding pastor was more traditional in his leadership style, which did not put a great emphasis on mission and vision. The past pastoral leadership places more emphasis on operating by a mission and vision through pastoral care, witnessing, and servicing the community. The first step was to establish a vision and mission by which the church should drive its services and resources thereby promoting an upswing in the lifecycle. As a result of this method most of the traditional and older, working class members had never witnessed a change as progressive minded as this newly appointed leadership team.

The creation of a new vision and mission statement were necessary to reverse the church's current fate, and begin its transformation. The goal was to deliver a clear picture to the church body, surrounding communities and other stakeholders as to the direction our church. As for the more traditional congregation at the time, change was not so easy to digest.

In the process of reviewing The Greater Piney Grove Baptist Church's shift, it is crucial to look at both the leader of this new church and the congregation of the "old church" and what caused such a fall. By digging deeply and looking across time, it became clearer that culture played a part in the shift and re-establishing phases of this church.

At the first sight of change, the veteran and more traditional congregants were not comfortable with having a Senior Pastor that was significantly younger than his predecessor. In addition, the Senior Pastor's leadership team was also younger and brought to the table fresh and new ideas, alongside transformation. This was a period of The Greater Piney Grove Baptist Church being very forward thinking and progressive natured in mission to move the dynamics of our church upward, onward, and forward. Serving on the leadership team as the Executive Pastor, our new roadmap came with a new set of standards and desires to build the congregation with a blend of young, middle class families which would carry the church's vision into the future, while being a comfortable fit in mirroring the community in which our church was stationed.

In the quest to get a true depiction of the effects of culture and the various functions it played in the transformation of The Greater Piney Grove Baptist Church, interviews and thoughtful discussion amongst myself and other church members commenced. While analyzing the dynamics our shifting church, it became clearer that the members and the new Senior Pastor were from different socio-economic backgrounds and age groups. This presented barriers as it relates to cultural differences. In assisting the Senior Pastor to bridge the gap of age and socio-economic cultural differences, the leadership team did ponder questions very similar to those presented by George Thompson Jr. in *Treasures in Clay Jars: New Ways to Understand Your Church*. In looking at culture intently, culture is defined as "deep, wide and complex."[10] The author of *Treasures in Clay Jars* also suggests that culture is that of learned and shared kind's human behavior.[11] Conducting interviews with members allowed for the gathering of general assumptions from those who endured the transitional years of a shifting church to the re-established church. It was interesting to record and analyze how they viewed the "patterned way of life" shared by the group of people that grew together and this newly re-established church family and congregation. Nevertheless, the class and age differences made this work very complex. In an effort to eliminate an even bigger shift in membership due to the cultural changes, Edgar Schein, author of *Organizational Culture and Leadership*, supports that leaders "must

---

[10] George B. Thompson, Jr., *Treasure in Clay Jars: New Ways to Understand Your Church*, (Cleveland: Pilgrim Press, 2003), 43-45.

[11] Ibid.

learn to decipher cultural cues so that normal flow of work is not interrupted by cultural misunderstandings."[12]

In looking at all of the dynamics that existed within our church culture, I took the lead in bridging the gap between the age, class, and tradition of the veteran members with the influx of new members that we had begun to draw and engage from the community. In reading *Treasures in Clay Jars*, I would compare my founding principles of family to those mentioned by Thompson, who introduces the image of congregation as a village.[13] As Executive Pastor, I wanted to implement effective practices and strategies that would allow for everyone in the congregation to have a common worship experience, regardless of age, class and/or forms of tradition. In working with Thompson's view of culture, I wanted to achieve a cultural balance within the church that supports a church that reflects "a patterned way of life shared by a group of people."[14] In looking at confluence, as Executive Pastor, I was instrumental in streaming together the divides that existed amongst the congregation.

The new leadership brought about a new vision and mission to drive the church forward in becoming a rising and re-established church. In looking at the location of our church and the effects of subculture, I creatively sought to merge the veteran members and the new members together who had been drawn by new ministries and the mission and vision of the church. In reading *Treasures in Clay Jars,* I now know

---

[12] Edgar H. Schein, *Organizational Culture and Leadership*, 3rd Edition, (San Francisco: Jossey-Bass, 2004; a Wiley imprint), 170.
[13] George B. Thompson, Jr., *Treasure in Clay Jars: New Ways to Understand Your Church*, (Cleveland: Pilgrim Press, 2003), 55.
[14] Ibid, 56

that my recognizing the need for balance among the multiple subcultures that existed aided the re-established phase of the church's lifecycle. Embracing these cultural differences and streaming balance between them allowed our new leadership to really focus on strengthening the ministry work that was a priority in the leadership of The Greater Piney Grove Baptist Church. In my outlook to change the divides and embrace the confluence of our congregation, I was looking for some shared assumptions, under which the congregation could function in worship and ministry as solid and whole. Although it took many years of holding onto this notion, shared assumptions are seamless and evident by a "village" spirit among the congregation. Schein supports the time it took to derive shared assumptions by asserting that, "in any given organization, shared assumptions arise only over a course of time and common experience."[15] With my focus being to engage congregants old and new in common experiences of worship, I was seeking to lead our church from declining to the dynamic phase of its lifecycle in allowing our mission and vision to really speak to our purpose as a church and ministry to each other and those surrounding us as well.

In looking at how George Thompson utilizes the swamp as a model of the many layers that exist within a church's culture, I was able to look at this model and study the power in using the swamp model, which presents the reader with a set of tools for examining our church. In the book, *How to Get Along with Your Pastor,* it explicitly develops how the "cultural swamp explains elements of your church's life that are

---

[15] Edgar H. Schein, Organizational Culture and Leadership, 3rd Edition, (San Francisco: Jossey-Bass, 2004; a Wiley imprint), 170

often missed.[16] After careful review of the model, I found it to be very helpful during reflection. The swamp model allowed me to understand the various phases, which The Greater Piney Grove Baptist Church went through. This model gave me an overall focus on balances and changes over time. In looking at the fluctuations in the course of change at The Greater Piney Grove Baptist Church, the new leadership positioned itself to a steadily progressive church.

Although my vision, alongside the leadership team's vision, was progressive, I wanted the veteran members to also embrace the change that was rapidly bringing The Greater Piney Grove Baptist back to speed and close to the dynamic phase at this point. In taking The Greater Piney Baptist Grove Baptist Church to the next level, I would seek to infuse new technology that was lacking and allow this to drive us from the dynamic phase to the re-established phase.

As Executive Pastor, the first step was to find common ground among the multiple subcultures that existed in the church. In continuous elevation through the church's lifecycle, a key leader that supported my efforts of moving our church to greater heights reminded me that going against one subculture's or set of norms and values was extremely risky. Indeed in seeking a medium, there were stages to go through in order to see the polished and finished product. My approach was not to ignore the norms and values of the more traditional and veteran members, but to infuse new initiatives and implement state-of the art technology that would ultimately move The Greater Piney Grove Baptist Church at a faster pace socially.

---

[16] George B. Thompson, Jr., *How to Get Along With Your Pastor: Creating Partnership for Doing Ministry*, (Cleveland: Pilgrim Press, 2006), 23-25.

In bridging a more traditional church in its primary years to a church that mirrored the progressive nature of the community and also inclusive of the time period in which we were living, the new vision and mission required building relationships. This allowed me to creatively merge the use of technology as a social forum in enhancing our worship services, routine activities and experiences, and was the start of building a new church. I was hopeful that this model could be a reflection of the congregation and the community in sync with the values and vision of the Senior Pastor and his leadership team. Ultimately, by presenting progressive cutting edge technology, we unleashed the boundaries, which led to a boost in membership growth.

A congregation that was first settled and happy about the traditional format of service and worship and was not functioning as a group that was futuristic in thinking. In the beginning stages of change in the church culture, the congregation was convinced that in order to expand numerically, the church had to be cohesive and accept a more contemporary worship format as opposed to the traditional model. Consequently, the new order of worship was accepted in a closed meeting. Yet the new worship structure was met with heavy resistance and profound hesitation from core members who understood the necessity of a modern-day church for relevancy and survival. However their future possibilities state of mind hindered progress towards the new vision and future possibilities. Being able to clearly depict the value of changing our direction and focus to becoming forward thinking and moving as a church was my task as a leader of The Greater Piney Grove Baptist Church. As the Executive Pastor, it was my desire to keep The Greater Piney Grove Baptist Church relevant and moving toward a vision of *"The Church With Help Hands,"* to all those who entered its doors.

Interestingly, Rev. William Flippin, Sr. in the same spirit of Rev. Jones saw there were needs and incorporated various ministries for the building of this spiritual kingdom for development and growth. These aspirations included: the initiation of the first annual revival (Fasting and Praying Week) in 1990 and continuing the annual revival week; the formation of the Montez Jones Evangelistic Circle, which is named in honor of the late Rev. Frank Jones' wife, to help evangelize the surrounding community; the restructuring of the Mission Department, and helping to secure a van for the transportation of senior citizens to weekly bible study. To further expand in the future, Pastor Flippin developed the Drama Department, Busy Bee Senior Citizens, Audio/Visual Media Ministry, New Members Training, Children and Youth Church and S.T.E.P. (Self Help for Teenage Pregnancy), to name a few.

In bringing about change, there were members who exhibited what George Thompson refers to as "stuff in the mud."[17] Since the veteran members had been without leadership and functioned strictly out of tradition for almost a year, it was a little overwhelming for them as they were fearful of such massive changes. They were also resistant by not being vocal, or expressing any excitement about the new progressive changes that were taking place in the leadership. The enhancement and current additions became the driving medium for extended viewing and the most current technology experiences. In analyzing our particular

---

[17] George B. Thompson, Jr., *Treasure in Clay Jars: New Ways to Understand Your Church*, (Cleveland: Pilgrim Press, 2003), 67-68.

subculture(s), the tension and anxiety of not being accustomed to change was in full display. *In How to Get Along with Your Pastor,* George B. Thompson suggests that perhaps this reaction was more normal than I understood; He adds, "submerged beliefs" become what they are as a result of its experiences."[18]

It took years for me to break through their shared assumptions that tradition was sufficient and change must not include the use of complicated equipment. In turn I set out to prove that not only was a serious transformation needed but also that the church was years behind in many aspects when our leadership first came aboard. The reality was that since the young adult, young family subculture began to dominate our membership, the church surely was driving on a mission to retention. The reality reflected in the present community as it began to blossom as a subculture within our congregations was that we had to remain current and keep focused on the future. Schien supports that a fundamental part of every culture is a set of assumptions about what is real and how one determines or discovers what is real."[19]

Furthermore, in analyzing the research and data gathered, The Greater Piney Grove Baptist Church experienced the cultural shore of the swamp over twenty years ago when it was without a pastor or formal leadership. The church suffered tremendously during this time period. Even without a pastor one would expect certain rituals and ordinances still be observed. However, most observable activities did not happen

---

[18] Thompson, George B., Jr., *How to Get Along with Your Pastor: Creating Partnership for Doing Ministry,* (Cleveland: The Pilgrim Press, 2006), 10.

[19] Edgar H. Schein, *Organizational Culture and Leadership,* 3rd Edition, (San Francisco: Jossey-Bass, 2004; a Wiley imprint), 140.

regularly and effectively such as: "worship services, Sunday school and educational programs, fellowship activities and outreach ministries." As a result of these rituals not taking place, the church declined. Unfortunately, this lack of leadership led to the downgrade of values and the core purpose that the church was ultimately putting forth.[20] The result of the swamp like characteristics that mired this church was a declining church with slack membership, very little structure and loss of vision, mission, and purpose.

To aid in re-establishing this declining church, we identified a common characteristic shared by both the declining of re-established church namely a family structured and family guided approach. The incoming Senior Pastor built from this family centered model a fresh approach to presenting values and purpose in the church. In re-establishing the values and purpose for the institution, a major goal was for this church to rise again. As suggested by author, George Thompson Jr., Pastor William E. Flippin, Sr. emphasized such instruments to help navigate the church to a higher ground.

As result of new leadership and a new pastor, it became evident that the cultural framework of The Greater Piney Grove Baptist Church needed to be addressed. The pastor's focus was to present solid "theologies and spiritual aspirations" to guide a sturdy re-established and flourishing church. Accordingly, the pastor's notion was met with little resistance. Many supported the pastor's approach of introducing a contemporary paradigm and pious objectives in the re-establishment of the church. A balanced congregation was a deliberate effort of Pastor Flippin's from

---

[20] Thompson, George B., Jr., *How to Get Along with Your Pastor: Creating Partnership for Doing Ministry*, (Cleveland: The Pilgrim Press, 2006), 23.

his inception to its current state. The new Senior Pastor took precise steps in taking this declining church to a higher standard of establishment and worship.

One of the largest dynamics, as it relates to culture, dealt with social class/occupational difference(s). In looking at the class structure of The Greater Piney Grove Baptist Church, under the leadership of Reverend Frank Jones, the congregation consisted of working class citizens. The social class of the congregation reflected the majority of the community. In looking at the temperament of the congregant, it was also reflective of the persona of Reverend Frank Jones. Reverend Jones' leadership style, which modeled that of "traditional authority," was very different from the new and current pastor. At the time the congregation was comfortable with only certain traditions and therefore, intimidated by change.

The earlier edifice, in which The Greater Piney Grove Baptist Church worshipped, was located in the heart of Metropolitan Atlanta. However, because of limited resources and social class, it operated like a very "traditional" rural black Baptist church. During the time of the declining church, when Reverend Jones expired, the church consisted of one service with a congregational make-up of between 500 and 1,000 congregants.

In making major changes, and re-establishing certain initiatives, Pastor William E. Flippin Sr., was able to offer a new vision that would inspire change over time and refuel The Greater Piney Grove Baptist Church in its mission and purpose in ministry. Simultaneous with the change of pastoral leadership, there was a visible shift in direction due to the values and economic class of the pastor.

The new pastor embodied an awareness of organizational wisdom about balancing, adaptability and manageability. Overtime, the older congregation blended with the new congregants that were attracted by the new pastor. Veteran members eventually embraced these new directions that would lead to a boost in church worship and transformational in the church's culture. The core members who weathered the period of decline in the church were "committed to working together and creating something new."[21]

The extent to which the church has blossomed reflects the present Senior Pastor as taking advantage of the "village like perspective." Taking this approach in the beginning phases of re-establishing The Greater Piney Grove Baptist Church was of great aid. The "village like approach" allowed Pastor William E. Flippin, Sr. to assess where the older congregation went wrong in its prior slump. He was then able to quickly assess those factors that assisted in the church's decline aside from the former pastor's death.[22]

One foundation that was actually built upon from the declining church was the value of the significance of family. This became the nuclear focus of re-establishing The Greater Piney Grove Baptist Church that exists today. Under Pastor William E. Flippin, Sr.'s leadership, a range of values and norms were established and set. Indeed, this effort

---

[21] George B. Thompson, Jr., *Treasure in Clay Jars: New Ways to Understand Your Church*, (Cleveland: Pilgrim Press, 2003), 87-92.

[22] Ibid.

produced a bond in the congregation that is a mix from the old church representing "the core who remained committed to working together and creating something new," blended with the new congregants that joined under the leadership of Pastor William E. Flippin, Sr.

Similarly, in harmonizing the tradition of a family atmosphere with a mission and service minded community church, the Senior Pastor, Senior Leadership and congregants cohesively agreed to preserve our interior values and conventional norms in the reconstruction phrase of the Greater Piney Baptist Grove Church. Author George Thompson, Jr., offers a clear purpose for the values and norms being established. Thompson offers that they are "Standards of behavior that are expected within a group to be taken seriously."[23] The bar was set high and this form of structure in setting standards for ministry, congregational life, and worship was now being taken seriously.

The shifts in the direction of the new leadership, a new building structure and culture changes in social class and occupation were very closely mirrored to the age and class of the Pastor Flippin Sr.. Although the Pastor's affluence was different from that of the former pastor and congregants, Pastor Flippin, Sr. infused new initiatives and found ways to ease the congregation while introducing certain rituals that would be necessary in re-establishing The Greater Piney Grove Baptist Church. Pastor William E. Flippin Sr. brought specific rituals to the new church. In time, the congregation moved from these rituals being modeled by the Senior Pastor to patterns of order shared by the congregants. These have now evolved into spiritual ceremonies of worship on Sunday.

---

[23] Ibid., 97-101.

Introducing these rituals was very important in re-establishing this declining church after he became pastor.[24]

In addition to the re-establishment of values, norms, rituals, and ceremonial changes taking place in The Greater Piney Grove Baptist Church to positively affect change, there was also the culture of class within the church. In the twenty years since 1990, The Greater Piney Grove Baptist Church's culture shifted in regards to its class and occupational culture under Pastor William E. Flippin Sr.. Interestingly, the culture shift of the church transpired mainly through its class with the fluctuation of new members who joined the church under Pastor Flippin's leadership. Twenty-years ago when Pastor Flippin became the church's fifth pastor, the leadership ethos of the church was shaped by mostly blue-collar hard workers, with modest traditional education, who conducted the day-to-day operations as a rural church in a metropolitan city. However, twenty years later due to expansion and statistical growth, The Greater Piney Grove Baptist Church reflects the friendly and charismatic persona and core values of Pastor William E. Flippin. These indications are great signs of leadership when any organization or church reflects the traditions, values, rituals and the personality of its leader. Similar to the personality of Pastor Flippin, twenty years later the church operates as an established and well-run church administratively in a metropolitan city with the emphases on discipleship not membership, spiritual growth and not personal gains. The church also emphasizes individual and church family values and conventional education.

---

[24] George B. Thompson, Jr., *Treasure in Clay Jars: New Ways to Understand Your Church*, (Cleveland: Pilgrim Press, 2003), 117-124.

Research suggests that in "the change of class it is almost inevitable that the factor of occupation of the congregants affect where people live and how they adapt." Indeed this new flare and change in the social class did affect our church.[25]

Therefore, within twenty years, The Greater Piney Grove Baptist Church changed as the result of the array of cultures that exists here and their concept of church. There has been a unified consensus throughout the church that it has evolved from a working class to more middle and professional class congregation. As a congregation and church family, The Greater Piney Grove is now, well rounded, diverse in service and services offered. The social culture of the church now has a more sculpted mission and emphasis, which encourage education and its benefit to a more progressive and transforming lifestyle. Because of the occupational culture shift that has taken place in the congregation, post the declining phase of the church; our church is now more community driven, social justice driven and family friendly.

Now at the re-establishing phase, The Greater Piney Grove Baptist Church is projected as a church that is more structured. The Senior Pastor has found ways to build on the strengths of the diverse sub-cultures, as they build upon one another, versus tearing the church apart. Our Senior Pastor, being a "charismatic authority model" was able to keenly design strategies to encourage the subcultures in our church to mix, blend and collaborate, rather than clinging too stubbornly to selfish and personal values or norms. In looking more closely at our Senior Pastor as the "charismatic authority model" he

[25] Thompson, George B., Jr., *How to Get Along with Your Pastor: Creating Partnership for Doing Ministry*, (Cleveland: The Pilgrim Press, 2006), 78-83.

was able to effectively articulate a high vision and called people to pursue it, demanding considerable commitment.[26]

In building upon these high visions, the structure of The Greater Piney Grove Baptist Church transitioned from the declining phase to the now re-established phase, operates smoothly with administrative leadership and a strong ministerial ministry only after twenty years, which included tension on all levels. Amidst recovering a church from the declining phase, other factors can be attributed to struggle, tension and tenacious pursuits to push through the climax of the culture change. In trudging through the climax of culture change, it took the Senior Pastor's strong influence and leadership skills to present a strong vision to move the church forward.

Also, in looking at the Senior Pastor's style and approach, he embodies a very strong resemblance to the "charismatic authority model." His personality and lifestyle also has a strong affect on the social class of people that were drawn to serve as members of this church. As a result of embracing tension as learning ground, the Senior Pastor was able to resolve the tension within sub-cultures, which in-turn led to expansion of our church. In pushing through the climax of culture change, it still took over twenty years for The Greater Piney Grove Baptist Church to build strong and respected foundations in values and norms to a now unified congregation and church family.

---

[26] George B. Thompson, Jr., *Treasure in Clay Jars: New Ways to Understand Your Church*, (Cleveland: Pilgrim Press, 2003), 117-124.

In seeking to progress and succeed in any futuristic goal, all leaders are defined by how they handle and triumph over their struggles, hardships, and tension. In reflection on the words of Frederick Douglass, "without struggle there is no progress."[27] The Senior Pastor's taking on the task of a declining church and reaching the climax of cultural change, and now to have a church operating on mission with six pillars of focus has been a testament to employing his vision and working his mission to glorify God. These are the six pillars and core values highlighted and stressed at The Greater Piney Grove Baptist Church:

FELLOWSHIP

This structure of this pillar is to demonstrate love and compassion for one another through various fellowship activities for the purpose of building unity in the body of Christ. The fellowship pillar is responsible for assisting people in their ability to grow spiritually as well as to love and connect with one another.

EVANGELISM/MISSION

This pillar evangelizes the lost and introduces unbelievers to the good news of Jesus Christ through existing outreach programs and ministries; through street witnessing efforts, etc. Further, the mission pillar provides refuge and services both locally and internationally for persons who are in need by providing local, emergency shelters for homeless women and children; and by providing schools and literacy

---

[27] Frederick Douglass, Goodreads-Quotable Quote, *Struggle and Progress*, http://www.goodreads.com/quotes/6398-if-there-is-no-struggle-there-is-no-progress-those=
(accessed March 4, 2014).

projects internationally. Further, it believes firmly that members are to have a mission's mentality that is reflected in the culture of our church.

WORSHIP

The worship pillar holds firm that the preached word is an essential biblical mandate and is essential to equipping the saints. Further, worshipping God in spirit and truth is central to bringing about a transformed life that glorifies God. And the worship experience must glorify God as members offer their gifts in sincere faith and obedience.

TEACHING

The biblical mandate of this pillar is to first become disciples and then to make disciples. The teaching of God's Word sets the stage for a transformed life. The teaching pillar emphasizes all leaders are to be engaged in a small group setting where the Word of God is taught and made applicable to this present age.

THE NEXT GENERATION MINISTRIES

The purpose of the Next Generation Ministries is to minister to families by providing a loving, Christ-Centered, learning environment for children, youth ranging in age from Kindergarten through 12th grade. The ministries core belief is that both our children, and youth will love God, grow in the grace and knowledge of our Lord and Saviour Jesus Christ and become living examples of Jesus Christ, ministering in the power of the Holy Spirit.

STEWARDSHIP

The premise of Stewardship is a shared, spiritual experience within The Greater Piney Grove Baptist Church family that involves the process of developing oneself spiritually so that you are able to give of yourself, one's spiritual gifts, a person's time, and a person's finances to building God's Kingdom. Thusly, Stewardship pillar encourages the church body to REASSESS their LIFESTYLES by taking a closer look at the different areas in their lives to discover a path to strengthen our relationship with God through one's personal sacrifice; to REARRANGE PRIORITIES by prayerfully considering one's contributions and reprioritizing a person's lives in accordance to God's will; and to REALLOCATE RESOURCES by individually and collectively shifting one's resources in acknowledgement that Stewardship is not about equal giving, but EQUAL SACRIFICE.

In re-establishing a declining church spanning more than twenty years, the Senior Pastor endured high tension in his pursuit to orderly address the cultural change of occupational class and social shift. It was made clear that even having a family centered focus and heart, that any established structure, be it family church, or corporate, that these structures will find face struggle. In conducting this case study, I looked intently at the different phases that The Greater Piney Grove went through to move its status from declining to the re-established.

The church's initial conflict lended itself to the clash of authority styles, although the new Senior Pastor operated in the "charismatic authority" model, not everyone else shared his leadership style. This conflict caused a rise in tension within subcultures, including key

42

leaders, administrators and shareholder members. Tension between different authoritative styles existed and had to be quickly brought under control. The desired relationship between the Senior Pastor, key leaders and shareholder members was not developing as hoped. The conflict was due to the key leaders and shareholder members operating under the model of "traditional authority" of the former pastor, whereas, the Senior Pastor operated in that of the model of "charismatic authority."

A common clash between these two different authority styles was inevitable. The Senior Pastor's charismatic authority model is to seek a win-win for all parties by gaining the cultural capital of the former leader's regime while still displaying a bureaucratic form of authority. This model was directly in conflict with the cultural capital and advantages of our Senior Pastor's charismatic authoritative model. These different operations of authority entered in a non-communication and non-productive time period in the mission of re-establishing the declining church.

However, as this tension of authority arose, the Senior Pastor quickly used his leadership skills to restructure the existing sub-cultures, setting a high vision for the sub- cultures to govern themselves through mission and purpose, versus that of personal issues of conflict. The highlight of the Senior Pastor's strategy to strengthen the streams of sub-cultures was to set forward mission on relationship building.

In compliment to the now and newly re-established congregation and occupational class change, the Senior Pastor of The Greater Piney Grove Baptist Church is a very forward thinking man of God. This aids Greater Piney Grove in being a church that is open to the possibilities of growth without much hindrance due to personal agendas or even cultural clashes. Despite the previous leadership regime being a blend of the "bureaucratic and traditional" models of authority, new structures of leadership have been developed consisting of key leaders and shareholder members who have now witnessed new success and heights in the plight to move a declining church to a re-established church.

The re-established nucleus and leadership now operating under our Senior Pastor's authoritative model can now be viewed as more trusting, respectful, open to communication, having a cohesive relationship, and the confidence to share power among the core leadership and administration. This newer leadership team, administration, and spiritual leaders of this newly re-established church focuses on what is best for its church body and its surrounding communities. It would be an error to omit that all these phases of tension and rough episodes and struggles led a common core and authority style in the re-establishing of The Greater Piney Grove Baptist Church.

Presently, due to a leveled and common ground-enveloping blend of cultural climate these struggles are now very manageable to the Senior Pastor. Now over time, finding balance amidst a stream of cultures is not as overwhelming. In twenty years of building relationships, gaining cultural capital, and overcoming people opposition, and the addition of ministerial programs, our Senior Pastor has set out on a vision to create a re-established church with a welcoming and very inviting atmosphere.

In addition, Pastor William E. Flippin Sr. dedicated over twenty years to working steadily to redirect, redefine, and re-establish this declining church into a new dynamic of the re-established church with a still growing membership. This membership now reflects the occupational class and social shift in class as the newly, re-established Greater Piney Grove Baptist Church reflects its surrounding community. In essence, a community which has shifted culturally and in social class; and now after witness of all the low and the dynamics of a declining church, the Senior Pastor has stood strong and faithful in the commitment of re-developing and re-establishing this institution and edifice for the Kingdom.

In view of the social class shift, alongside the building upon the sub-cultures that exist within our congregation, this Senior Pastor has led in the expansion of being able to service more people to God. In doing so, The Greater Piney Grove Baptist Church has now expanded from having only one worship service to two church worship opportunities. In serving three services, in both evangelical and contemporary style services, our Senior Pastor now serves and shepherds approximately 2,500 active congregational church family members.

In looking at this case study of the declining church to the re-established church, data collected highlights that within this twenty plus years span of change, re-building and re-establishing this church, its congregation, its ministries, mission and vision were only successful after ushering in change. The Senior Pastor, however, in issuing forth change made it a priority to stay in touch and tuned into factors that did, would, and possibly could affect our church's progression.

In being conscious of the shifts in culture and working through the climax of this culture change, he stood firm on values, norms, rituals, and even symbols in his effort to re-establish a declining church. From the beginning, the Senior Pastor, even through the shift of culture change as it relates to occupational culture, kept focus. His foundations of evangelism, worship, mission, teaching, and fellowship were clear and firm as he delivered to the people he shepherds. In settling this ground in the focuses of ministry of The Greater Piney Grove Baptist Church, under his leadership, he deemed and set these as the six pillars of the church.

In being a tenacious and steadfast pastor and leader, this vision was initially the vision that he projected for the church. Now, post declining and even post climax of the culture change, in keeping with his core beliefs as pastor and modeling charismatic authority approach, over time has called people to pursue it and called for commitment, evangelism, worship, mission, teaching, stewardship and fellowship to his focus. Now the church and community have embraced these six pillars without resistance. As a result, it is evident that our church is now on one accord in the newly re-established phase of the church's life cycle.

The case study reveals that the congregation now, post the declining phase resembles that of the image of our Senior Pastor. In view of the social change of our congregation as it relates to occupational class, it resembles very closely that of the Senior Pastor's education, administrative strengths, command of order, knowledge of policy and structure; and speaks to the caliber of occupational culture that exists within the re-established Greater Piney Grove Baptist Church.

Now, as a church body, The Greater Piney Grove Baptist Church seems to be flowing in the same direction. In the Senior Pastor slating the foundation for a common purpose, the church has truly revitalized and transitioned to a more solid foundation. In the context of cultural confluence, our church has become more mission driven. As one of this church's six pillars, The Greater Piney Grove Baptist Church is now taking to greater heights in mission to move ministry beyond the walls of its physical setting.

In re-establishing the declining church, the Senior Pastor also imprinted the vision of fellowship and family on the minds and in the hearts of his congregation. In an effort to strengthen cultural streams that exist within the church and in strengthening the bond amongst different sub-cultures within the church, our Senior Pastor drew on his personal love for family and projected these values into his church. Again, asserting a "high vision and calling people to pursue it" and now our church is very family oriented.[28]

In servicing a congregation family style, the Greater Piney Grove Baptist Church has expanded its building structure to accommodate its family members with a new addition of a balcony, a new contemporary worship style and format, two worship services, a Family Life Center and a new state-of-the-art sanctuary all on our church campus.

---

[28] George B. Thompson, Jr., *Treasure in Clay Jars: New Ways to Understand Your Church*, (Cleveland: Pilgrim Press, 2003), 137-143.

Chapter 2.

The 21st Century Baptist Church Model of Leadership Through Relationship, Spiritual Covenant and Mentorship

"Good leaders must first become good servants."[29]

-Robert Greenleaf

WHAT IS LEADERSHIP IN THE 21ST CENTURY CHURCH

The twenty-first century African American Baptist Church is acknowledged by the power of leadership and its influence as a Christian institution. Many pastors build a faithful league of followers through charismatic preaching, traditional teachings, contemporary worship, community involvement, and religious persuasion. Establishing a church culture that effectively attracts, equips and empowers young adults to assume leadership positions in a traditional culture has plagued the social blueprint of many current church leadership paradigms. As a result of this hindrance, the twenty-first century church in particular African American Baptist Church's have been asked many lingering questions regarding effectiveness of leadership in the present-day Christian movement. Thereby, it has caused the universal question to be raised not only from modern day parishioners but also from pastors alike, "How can a successful leader develop quality leadership models with Young Adult Christians constituency?"

---

[29] Robert Greenleaf, *Servant Leadership Quotes Put Others First,* http://www.youreffectiveleadership.com/servant-leadership-quotes.html (accessed March 13, 2014).

In order to answer this question, one must first define how today's church can persuade young potential leaders to accept influential positions. Modestly, the twenty-first century leader in any church context is portrayed as practically, "An individual that influences a group of followers to achieve a common goal."[30] Therefore, to effectively cultivate the environment for young leaders to take on leadership positions successfully, there always has to be an achievable and common goal by an influential leader. This achievable and established means is through relationship, spiritual covenant, and mentorship. In an attempt to thoroughly develop this theory, three exemplars of leadership theory will be presented to help cultivate characteristics of leadership empowerment that can be used to establish young adult involvement. These characteristics are as follows: Servant Leadership, Leadership Development, and the Cultural Dynamics of Leadership.

SERVANT LEADERSHIP

What is Servant Leadership? The book entitled *Servant Leadership* by Efrain Agosto identifies servant leadership through the guidance of Paul towards Timothy and many of his faithful young followers.[31] The Pauline type of leadership evokes followers to lead with a servant's heart. This is evident when Paul consistently urges and writes to Timothy, from prison that the qualification of servant *diokonos* leadership within the church where one must be well-thought-of, committed, humble, and not use their position to go to their head or

---

[30] Kenneth Boulding, *Concept of Leadership*,
http://www.nwlink.com/~donclark/leader/leadcon.html (accessed October 20, 2013).
[31] Efrain Agosto, *Servant Leadership: Jesus & Paul*, (St. Louis: Chalice Press, 2005), 12.

cause confusion in the church.[32] Paul concludes his advice to Timothy by stating, "Those who do this servant work will come to be highly respected, a real credit to this Jesus-faith.[33]

Agosto agrees with Paul's prerequisite of servant leader when he highlights, "The great leader is seen as a servant first. The servant leader strives to make sure that other people's highest priority needs are being served. By meeting people's needs for growth and development the goals of a particular organization are being met."[34] Therefore, it is the responsibility of current church leaders to foster a Christian environment wherein serving is the vision and mission of the church. Most importantly, when the servant leader places serving others as primary it will permeate the cultural atmosphere while modeling for the young adults the importance of being a servant leader and serving others.

Subsequently, senior leadership should always seek to cultivate young adult leaders who are currently being provided the model of servant leadership. In soliciting such a leader, the total spiritual wealth of the young adults must be taken into account. Senior leaders must develop this targeted group by encouraging their talents and being willing to follow relevant contemporary trends. By making it a point to invest service in this growing organization it will ensure future growth and change the social climate within the overall church setting. Implementation of such a model will require senior leaders to intently listen to and carry out where possible and meaningful the voices and

---

[32] 1 Timothy 3 (The Message Bible).
[33] 1 Timothy 3:13 (The Message Bible).
[34] Efrain Agosto, *Servant Leadership: Jesus & Paul*, (St. Louis: Chalice Press, 2005), p.

ideas of the young adult congregants in the areas of contemporary worship, promoting relevant Christian educational courses through the use of bible studies relating to young adult situations, and through integrating young adults as role models to minister to the next generation. By establishing this spiritual matrix, the church will develop a centripetal force framework whereby the culture of the church constantly revolves around the ultimate example of servant leader, Jesus Christ.

PRACTICING SERVANT LEADERSHIP

In an effort to create lasting change in the Baptist church culture, the ideal of servant leadership must move beyond the confines of a spiritual concept, and transcend into a practical spiritual decorum. In modern day theological settings, the trend of traditional practices, democratic control, and hierarchal archetypes are fluid throughout leadership structures. Present-day leadership styles should become more deliberate in emphasizing teamwork, ethical decision-making, and building stronger alliances among young adults who attend its church services. Once experienced leaders seek to promote the personal development of young adult believers in the congregation, the total worth and tone of the church will improve spiritually, numerically, and effectively. Ultimately, authentic servant leadership occurs when it is founded on the principle of service to others, the sole priority as a catalyst of servanthood before its parishioners.

In the context of today's church practices and leadership approaches, there are numerous definitions and explanations of both *servant* and *leader*. Nevertheless, when one closely evaluates the words "servant" and "leader" most would promptly detect that these two commonly used words are synonymous with each other, and yet each is the complete antithesis of the other. How so? When one merges these words to be utilized in a Christian setting both descriptive adjectives connect to become a synergistic phrase that reflects a Christian who is a servant first as Paul indicated to Timothy. This is indicated further in the writings of Peter when he connects the practice of servant leadership in relation to a Shepherd (pastor) serving faithfully God's flock (the congregation). Peter says, "Shepherd the flock of God which is among you, serving as overseers, not by compulsion but willingly, not for dishonest gain but eagerly; nor as being lords over those entrusted to you, but being examples to the flock; and when the Chief Shepherd appears, you will receive the crown of glory that does not fade away."[35]

Both the Apostles Paul and Peter would support Robert K. Greenleaf's stance on servant leadership practice that one must, "begin with the natural feeling that one wants to serve. Then conscious choice brings one to aspire to lead. The best test is: do those served grow as persons: do they, while being served, become healthier, wiser, freer, more autonomous, more likely themselves to become servants?"[36]

In an effort to capitalize on this spiritual concept as it translates into a practical spiritual norm there are a variety of essential qualities a

---

[35] 1 Peter 5:2-4 (NKJV).
[36] Robert K. Greenleaf. *"The Concept of Servant Leadership"* 16 (May 2002): 27, http://www.regent.edu/acad/global/publications/jvl/vol1_iss1/Spears_Final.pdf (accessed October 20, 2013).

servant leader must initially exhibit. These "key attributes" are as follows:

In the area of Relationship:

Listening- This term is defined as the act of attentively taking heed or paying attention to a conversation. In servant leadership, having the ability to disseminate between "receptive listening", reflection, and trusting in the overarching guidance of the Holy Spirit is essential in becoming a well-rounded servant leader.

Empathy- This can be seen as a leader's ability to recognize, and understand distinct emotions being experienced by another person. A servant leader is sensitive to the feelings and thoughts of another person's heart. Recognizing and accepting a person's uniqueness in spirit is a key aspect of truly being effective in this area.

In the Area of Spiritual Covenant:

Healing- This term is seen as a servant leader's ability to help one overcome carnal and spiritual afflictions through the use of biblical principles. Through the restorative use of healing scriptures, prayers, and spirit filled worship, the integrity of what was once deemed as broken can be made whole again. At some point in every believer's life the feeling of inadequacy and self-doubt will be experienced. It is the servant leader's charge to encourage and uplift the afflicted believer by directing him or her back to Gods words and promises.

Awareness- Is the ability to perceive or to be cognitively conscious of things and events occurring in a present state. As a servant leader, the ability to become spiritually in tune with the needs and concerns of the congregation is imperative. Fostering an open line of communication within the mentor mentee paradigm is crucial. Servant leaders should seek to reunite mentee's to a spiritual state of balance.

Conceptualization- Is the act of manifesting the unseen into a reality. Servant leaders in the area of conceptualization serve as visionary leaders to the congregation. By looking beyond the day-to-day nuances many leaders predicate this discipline through unwavering faith, daily reflection, and periodically fasting to stay spiritually in tune to the needs of the church.

In the Area of Mentorship

Commitments to the growth of people- Servant leaders understand that in order to permeate an environment for the growth of young leaders there is a keen responsibility to cultivate the personal development of workers within the church. In order to facilitate spiritual development, an atmosphere of accountability can be fostered in the social, emotional, and spiritual areas of the young adult's life.

Stewardship- Is a term used to describe the responsible planning and management of resources within God's kingdom. These resources include, but are not limited to, the dedication of a young adult's time, talent, and tenth in the house of God. A strategic plan must be implemented in order to show developing believers healthy ways to balance these spiritual areas.

Building Community- The term community can be expressed as a unifying feeling of fellowship with others in the areas of spiritual beliefs, goals, and religious values. Upon building community the young adult population must become vested in the ideal of growth towards a common goal. Servant leaders can help to cultivate this sense of community through church organizational groups. These groups allow stewards to become active members in church culture.

LEADERSHIP DEVELOPMENT

According to the author John C. Maxwell, cultivating an atmosphere of integrity and self- discipline is a quintessential component for developing authentic leadership. The author suggests that there are five levels in helping to foster an authentic leader:

Level 1: Position

Level 2: Permission

Level 3: Production

Level 4: People Development

Level 5: Personhood/ Respect[37]

When seeking authentic leadership and going through the five levels indicated by John Maxwell above, one must ask the question is *"leadership"* a type of personality character trait? Are people innately born with the ability to lead? In an effort to expand the development of future young adult leaders, existing pastors must understand the complexities of these questions in order to seek out qualified perspective young adult leaders. The most accurate definition of leadership, as mentioned at the onset, is the level of influence a person

---

[37] John C.Maxwell, *Developing The Leader Within You*, (Nashville: Thomas Nelson, 1993), 15-16.

has over a set group of people. Leadership guru, John Maxwell, sums it up best in discussing the level of influence, "He who thinketh he leadeth and hath no one following him is only taking a walk."[38] Having a sincere appreciation for the levels to which one can influence the body of Christ is the core of developing a young adult leader. Maxwell further states, "Once you define leadership as the ability to get followers, you work backwards from that point of reference to figure out how to lead."[39] The novice thinker would associate position with authentic leadership; however, while this essential element is vital to leadership and influence the key component required is acquiring a dedicated group of followers. In short, prospective servant leaders should be open to the ideal of expanding their level of influence.

Increasing Levels of Influence:

How does one increase the level of influence personally and among others? One, a person must accept the plausibility that everyone has influence and can persuade others. Indeed, prospective young adult leaders should be aware that every individual leads in some capacity every day as Luke writes, "Be on guard for yourselves and for all the flock, among which the Holy Spirit has made you overseers, to shepherd the church of God which He purchased with his own blood."[40] Maxwell affirms writer Luke's suggestion by highlighting that, "The issue is not whether you influence someone. What needs to be settled is what kind of influencer you will be."[41] While many may

---

[38] Ibid.,1.

[39] Ibid., 2.

[40] Acts 20:28 (CSB).

[41] John C. Maxwell, *Developing The Leader Within You*, (Nashville: Thomas Nelson, 1993)., 4.

not have confidence in the level of influence they have upon others, individuals should stand assured that influence is a skill that can be developed over time. In the book entitled *Power and Influence,* author Robert Dilenschneider states that there are three components to leadership, "The three components of this triangle are communication, recognition, and influence. You start to communicate effectively. This leads to recognition and recognition in turn leads to influence."[42] In an effort to take a hard-nosed approach to the explicit characteristics of influence the basic principles of leadership development will now be outlined.

In the Area of Relationship:

Position/ Rights- This influential level is when people follow you because they have to. This is a result of one being either appointed or elected in this authoritative position. Unfortunately, the only authority one has is what a leader's office title gives a person. Regrettably, the longer a person stays at the *position right level*, the higher the turnover rate and the lower the morale of the people.[43] Within this tier of influence, future young adult leaders must begin to develop a lasting relationship within their prospective aspirant. This level of leadership is deemed as the lowest level of effectiveness. By placing a higher emphasis on title, an individual on this level will not mature beyond the confines of their job description. In an effort to circumvent this reality, young adult leaders must push beyond their level of title and assert confident authority. These are the qualities needed to be successful within the level of position and rights:

---

[42] Ibid.,5.
[43] John C. Maxwell, *The 360-Degree Leader* (Nashville, TN: Thomas Nelson, 2005),58.

- Know your job description thoroughly.
- Be aware of the history of the organization.
- Relate the organization's history to the people.
- Accept responsibility.
- Do your job with consistent excellence.
- Do more than expected.
- Offer creative ideas for change and improvement.[44]

Permission/ Relationships- At this junction, people follow you because they want to. In other words, people follow the leader beyond one's stated authority.   Trust is indeed being established between leaders and followers; however, misgivings are still present. The *permission and relationship* style begins to be purposeful and meaningful with some reservations.[45]   Further, this particular level of influence can be outlined as a leader who attempts to develop followers in connection to a "pecking order" paradigm. Reflecting an emergent leadership approach, this level of influence is based on developing a descending hierarchy of interrelationships within a group. Persons within this stance of influence have a tendency to be product oriented. In an effort to avoid leading through intimidation, Maxwell denotes "Leadership begins with the heart, not the head. People don't care how much you know until they know how much you care. People who are unable to build solid, lasting relationships will soon discover that they are unable to sustain long, effective leadership."[46] Maxwell emphasizes

[44] Pat Riley, *The Winner Within,* (New York: Berkley Publishing, 1994), 41-45.
[45] John C. Maxwell, *The 360 Degree Leader* (Nashville, TN: Thomas Nelson, 2005), 5.
[46] John C. Maxwell, *Developing The Leader Within You,* (Nashville: Thomas Nelson, 1993)., 7-8.

even further these are the qualities needed to be successful within the level of permission and relationship:

- Possess a genuine love for people.
- Make those who work with you more successful.
- See through other peoples' eyes.
- Love people more than procedures.
- Do "win-win" or don't do it.
- Include others in your journey.
- Deal wisely with difficult people.[47]

In the Area of Spiritual Covenant:

Production/ Results- This identifies people who follow a leader because of what one has done for the organization. This level emphasizes that people sense godly success for the church. This is when the relationship is established between leader and follower because of their overall production within and outside the church. Interestingly, this is where most leaders have a genuine sense of success, and likewise, their followers pick up a sense of fulfillment in participating. Plainly, the church has accepted the leader as a respected figure who speaks on their behalf because of his/her accomplishment at the institution.[48]

Further, this level of influence is indicative of achieving a sense of success through a well-esteemed track record. Upon embarking on this

---

[47] Ibid., 15.
[48] John C. Maxwell, *The 360-Degree Leader* (Nashville, TN: Thomas Nelson, 2005), 5.

level of influence an undeniable push of momentum is formed based upon elevated morale and goals being attained. Moreover a results oriented style of leadership is delineated. Young adult leaders within this level do not have to be qualified in order to truly be effective. These are the qualities established to be successful in the level of production and results:

- Initiate and accept responsibility for growth.
- Develop and follow a statement of purpose.
- Make job description and energy an integral part of purpose.
- Develop accountability for results, beginning with yourself.
- Know and do the things that give a high return.
- Communicate the strategy and vision of the organization.
- Become a change agent and understand timing.
- Make the difficult decisions that will make a difference.[49]

In the Area of Relationship:

People Development/ Reproduction- Functioning under the notion of the African proverb "It takes a village," influence is merely a reflection of a leader's ability to empower others. This integral stage focuses on the level of loyalty young adult constituents will have if shepherded under the right leadership model. Young adult prospective leaders follow because of the leaders' impact on them personally and spiritually. Because of the leaders' effect on them, this begins an established relationship, continual mentorship, and most importantly,

---

[49] Samuel R. Chand, *Who's Holding Your Ladder?* (Niles, IL: Mall Publishing, 2003)., 35-45.

long-range growth. The *people development and reproduction* juncture is the commitment to produce leaders by insuring constant growth to the church and to individuals.[50]

Undergirding workers with the confidence to attain personal growth through strategic instruction and exceptional advancement are by-products of quality leadership. These are the attributes needed to be successful within the level of people development and reproduction:

- Realize that people are your most valuable asset.
- Place a priority on developing people.
- Be a model for others to follow.
- Pour your leadership efforts into the top 20 percent of your people.
- Expose key leaders to growth opportunities.
- Be able to attract other winner/ producers to the common goal.
- Surround yourself with an inner core that compliments your leadership.[51]

Personhood/ Respect- The final stage of influence is through the means of relationship, spiritual covenant and mentorship. In the decisive paradigm phase, many will have spent years growing both people and church. Particularly, people follow because of the leader's integrity, authenticity, love, and talents.[52] The key aspect of influence within this level is the ideal of building a "Tried and True" leadership

---

[50] Samuel R. Chand, *What's Shakin' Your Ladder?* (Niles, IL: Mall Publishing, 2005)., 53-57.
[51]Samuel R. Chand, *Who's Holding Your Ladder?* (Niles, IL: Mall Publishing, 2003)., 40-45.
[52] Samuel R. Chand, *What's Shakin' Your Ladder?* (Niles, IL: Mall Publishing, 2005)., 58-62.

brand. One can define a brand as a distinguished characteristic categorizing a product or service. Young adult leaders who attain this level of achievement understand that the process required to stay within this paradigm often takes a lifetime to achieve. Normally, few individuals achieve this level of influence due to death. Often their influence out lasts their life's work. These are the qualities needed to be successful in the level of personhood and respect:

- Your followers are loyal and sacrificial.
- You have spent years mentoring and molding leaders.
  You have become a statesman/ consultant, and are sought out by others.
- Your greatest joy comes from watching others grow and develop.
- You transcend the organization.[53]

---

[53] John C. Maxwell, *Developing The Leader Within You*, (Nashville: Thomas Nelson, 1993)., 16.

THE CULTURAL DYNAMICS OF LEADERSHIP

The culture dynamics of any institution are essential to effective leadership. For each culture foretells the history, suffering, value, story, triumphs, and even defeats of an organization. In this case, the culture dynamics is the DNA, the lifeline of the church and it is very important to its future growth. To be a successful leader in reshaping the social climate and to inspire others to lead it is crucial for one to study, understand and navigate the culture elements of the church they serve.

Whenever one analyzes the social climate of the church, an individual must ask, "What is the culture dynamics of leadership in relation to the church?" International leadership guru, Samuel R. Chand best proffers this line of thinking; he maintains that when a leader develops a strong vibrant culture and environment, success is eminent. Further, when the leader stimulates and encourages others to not only do better but be better, the organization will prosper. Consequently, the motivation is for people to rise so that they can reach their highest and full potential.[54]

Therefore, it is the responsibility of the spiritual leader to not only show the way, point the way forward, but to also train others to be an active participant in developing and reshaping the church culture. When a leader does this, it renovates a healthy culture by integrating resources to equip, inspire and transform potential leaders to serve the church and the community alike. Chand further suggests to successfully alter the

---

[54] Samuel R. Chand. *Cracking Your Church's Culture Code: Seven Keys to Unleashing Vision & Inspiration* (San Francisco: Jossey-Bass, 2011), 4.

culture dynamics of the church, the leader must focus on the potential leader's heart and character and not their resume or ability.[55] Paul even urges Timothy on the importance of the probable leader's spirit and attributes in the Christian church. Paul says to Timothy, "One must also have a good reputation with outsiders, so that they will not fall into disgrace and into the devil's trap."[56]

Upon evaluating the term culture, many theologians perceive this phrase as the most powerful determining factor within any organization. Culture predicates whether or not an existing trend or ideal will be accepted upon presentation, or refuted based on staunch assumptions. Morale, cohesiveness, flexibility, and teamwork models are indicative of the cultural strategy fluently being used in the church. Church culture, not vision, will determine the extent of progressive development a church can make within a given amount of time. Chand suggests, "Many leaders confuse culture with vision and strategy, but they are very different. Vision and strategy usually focus on products, services, and outcomes but culture is about the people, the most valuable asset in the organization."[57] In an effort to explore the cultural health of the church, prospective young adult leaders must take into account the integrity of the vision casters. The level of virtue under which a leader presides can be reflected in the intensity of ministerial proxies developed by a pastor. Do these prospective leaders share identical precepts, goals, values upon which the ministry abides? A

---

[55] Ibid., 49.
[56] 1 Timothy 3:7 (NIV)
[57] Samuel R. Chand. *Cracking Your Church's Culture Code: Seven Keys to Unleashing Vision & Inspiration* (San Francisco: Jossey-Bass, 2011), 4.

litmus test can be given to gauge whether the current staff and administrative teams are seeking growth or merely pontificating ritualistic ideas. There are ten precursors that can be identified which will hinder the visionary progression of the contemporary church's cultural development. These elements are as follows:

Limited Leaders- Leaders that qualify within this category lack a clear vision. These individuals are unable to see the big picture and irrefutably operate under a self-centered style of leadership; making the focus of the cultural atmosphere about the leader, as opposed to developing a core group of faithful workers.

Concrete Thinkers- This term can be defined as a developmental thing in a very literal way. This type of thinker is unable to conceptualize the vision given in conjunction with the future and can only focus on situations happening in the now.

Dogmatic Talkers- These individuals can be described as having very strong negative opinions about a situation or ideal. Often dogmatic individuals assert themselves as the end all authority in an area and will not take no for an answer. They can habitually make assumptions about a circumstance with no evidence to support their ideal.

Satisfied Sitters- Church affiliates who embody this character trait are individuals who are most comfortable in a predictable setting. These lay-members seek out non-threatening interactions and do not like to become engaged beyond their comfort zone.

Tradition Lovers- This type of parishioner is vested in the continuation of ancestral practice. Despite modern day innovations a tradition lover cannot see beyond the tides of yesteryear's nostalgias.

Census Takers- These groups of individuals are uneasy about thinking outside of the box. The ideals of the majority in charge are the only ideals they are willing to embrace. Utilizing the philosophy of "majority rules" as their motto, these individuals actively seek out other people with common values and opinions before making a decision.

Problem Perceivers- There are certain leaders who see a problem in every solution. These persons never enter into a circumstance with a resolution in mind. Problem perceivers wait for unfortunate situations to occur with the intent of being the mandated reporter.

Self Seekers- Constituents qualifying within this category are the "It's All About Me" believers. Never truly achieving a set goal, these individuals are highly self-centered and selfish.

Failure Forecasters- Often times this antagonistic group has an uncanny ability to always see the forecast as wet and gloomy. With an outlook of misguided despair and uncertainty these individual's often predict failure before it even occurs.

Continual Losers- These individuals live in a constant state of past experiences. Based on prior failures, the overwhelming sense of fear inhibits their ability to make sound decisions in the future. Like the "Little Engine that Could" these individuals should concentrate on pursuing constant forward movement. Somehow unable to manifest this reality these individuals also seek out ways to stunt other visionaries' growth productivity.

CULTURURAL DYNAMICS OF THE MODERN DAY CHURCH

Interestingly, in the article written by David A. Roozen, "A Decade of Change in American Congregations," he highlights the many sources of conflict in the modern-day church. It emphasizes that conflict or disagreement appears in significantly different aspects of congregational life; however, many of these traits are found in a majority of congregations. Initially, for many churches, tension occurs when the church enforces out-dated norms and traditional values when relevancy comes into question. Secondly, strain formulates in churches due in part to the self-centered, self-righteous and hypocritical behavior of churchgoers. Next, the style of worship plays a major part where it is designed to bring in the unity of the faith, yet it causes more disorder, disruption, and isolation from its congregants. Finally and most importantly, the reason culture dynamic differences occur is because of leadership styles and decision-making that discourage persons from attending church services.[58] So, what are we going to do to positively change the culture dynamics of a church's reputation?

This question can be answered best in a story about a man and the Alaskan Iditarod dogsled race. The Iditarod dogsled race is one of the most grueling and demanding challenges in the world. A team of dogs was pulling a heavy sled over rugged terrain in terrible Alaskan weather, struggling for days to be the first across the finish line. In an interview with an Iditarod winner, the reporter asked the secret of the dogsled driver's success. The driver shrugged and said, "I train each of

---

[58] David A. Roozen, Faith Communities Today Article, *A Decade of Change in American Congregations,* 25 (June 2010): www.faithcommunitiestoday.org. (accessed November 13, 2013).

the dogs to be a leader."[59]   Likewise this leadership approach should always be the forefront and the vision of the church's mission and goal, "to train each person to be a leader."   By doing so it will empower every member to pull together and share leadership while "running the race set before us."[60]

In an effort to progressively move toward a culturally dynamic church, future young adult leaders must operate under the sentiments that change is a constant reality. Often seen as the protagonist in the arena of life, change is the one constant that leaders can grow to depend on. Whether enhancing technological systems, diversifying ministerial staff, or updating facility locations, throughout a church's progression, change never ceases to occur. Having a keen understanding of cultural dynamics will help the ever-growing believer population transcend beyond the concept of utilizing change as a model to implementing transitionary strategies within the organization.   Transition can be defined as the internal transformation that occurs in the areas of emotional, financial, psychological, and relational church dynamics. Being equipped to realize the distinct difference between change and transition will help prospective church leaders effectively implement a transition strategy.

Transition management is a distinctive type of management style, which people often resist initially. Coming to terms with the prospect of new situations and uncontrollable external events is not always easy in a culturally progressive church. Allowing potential young adult

---

[59] Craig Brain Larson, 750 Engaging Illustrations for Preachers, Teachers and Writers, (Grand Rapids: Barker Books, 2007), 298.
[60] Hebrews 12:1 (KJV)

leaders to have insight into the manner in which the transition model will be implemented is the key. Being able to properly communicate the purpose, picture, plan, and parts of the transition strategy will evoke a level of confidence within leadership circles. Five key components needed in order to effectively implement this model are as follows:

- Develop and implement strategies for helping young adult leaders make a new beginning.

- Provide young adult leaders the opportunity to practice their newly developed skills.

- Work collaboratively with prospective young adult leaders to help define their new roles and practices.

- Reward structural practices that support new appropriate behavior, skills, and knowledge.

- Publicize and celebrate early successes.

- Build in responsiveness and flexibility to ensure continued adaptation to the changing environment.[61]

Given these points, active young adult involvement within ministerial sectors is progressively increasing, attaining young ministers with a heart for Christ helps to continue the vision of church leadership by staying true to traditional precepts while progressing towards contemporary ideals. In an effort to give a more pluralistic view of

[61] Jim McCarthy, Change Management versus Transition Management Article, 1 (June, 2011) http://www.jimmccarthyonline.com/2009/06/123/

leadership expectations, leadership styles under the traditional and the contemporary settings will provide prospective young adult leaders with diversified guidelines on leadership principles.

Chapter 3.

New Leadership-Equipping, Empowering and Energizing Others

"Jesus sent a clear message to all those who would follow Him that leadership was to be first and foremost an act of service. No plan B was implied or offered in His words."[62]

-Ken Blanchard

The concept of constructing a Leadership Development Plan began after The Greater Piney Grove Baptist Church reached the climax in the declining phase of a church's cycle. As a result of the decline, the Senior Pastor, Senior Leadership team, and I reached a critical point and had to pose the question to ourselves, "Do we stay at this point in the wilderness of content or continue to our destiny of the Promised Land through the means of developing vibrant leadership?" At this critical juncture the Senior Leadership team and I surrendered to the notion of change if we were going to continue to implement our mission and vision to future generations of the church. We unanimously agreed that an analysis was needed in the area of leadership, training Greater Piney Grove Baptist Church's *Strengths, Weaknesses, Opportunities,* and *Threats (S.W.O.T.)*. Our S.W.O.T. analysis was conducted over a two-month period.

Consequently, the purpose of the Leadership Development Plan is to provide concrete direction for the future so The Greater Piney Grove

---

[62] Ken Blanchard and Phil Hodges., *Lead Like Jesus: Lesson from The Greatest Role Model of All Time,* (Nashville: Thomas Nelson, 2005), 197.

Baptist Church is always strategically aligned with its mission and vision of creating an atmosphere to develop vital leaders. As result of the Leadership Development, leaders and members will be Redeemed to a personal relationship with Christ, Reconciled to God and His people, Restored to wholeness, to well-being, and Revived for a full life involved in service to others. The mission of The Greater Piney Grove Baptist Church is to provide refuge and services to improve the well being of all those in and connected with this church and the surrounding community. To be distinguished by our words and our deeds as *The Church With Helping Hands.* Thusly, the Leadership Development Plan is to provide a process for how the congregants will effectively carry out the mission of the church and grow spiritually and holistically. The Leadership Development Plan is accomplished when members invest in the mission of the church and are being a consistent and an active collaborator in the re-establishment fragment of the church.

The Greater Piney Grove Baptist Church's location provides prime opportunity for the church to conduct viable ministry activities in a diverse and growing community. The face of the local neighborhood has changed and now reflects a multi-class, multi-ethnic group of people who may or may not have united with a local church body. The Grove is now poised to carry out the mandate of Jesus Christ to go into this neighborhood and make disciples of people who do not necessarily represent the ethnic majority of our current membership.[63]

---

[63] Matthew 28:19 (New International Version)

The foundation of the Leadership Development Plan is based on the five-core pillars (Teaching, Fellowship, Mission, Evangelism, and Worship) of the Grove. The core values, goals, and strategies are all encompassed in these five core pillars of our church. While holding on to these basic concepts, the strategy plan orchestrates us to conduct ministries that are inclusive of all and more importantly, meets the needs of all our members through the five-core pillars. Implementation will take time, effort and cooperation from all our church leaders. However, the goals and strategies presented can be accomplished. All activities of the church, as we develop new leaders, will be pillar-based with the final goal of equipping both prospective leaders and the saints for the work of ministry, and for the edifying of the body of Christ.[64]

As a result of our leadership development, an S.W.O.T. analysis was used during planning that determined that a more comprehensive approach to leadership development was essential for the future growth, new leaders, and stability of ministerial functions. Indirectly, after the S.W.O.T. analysis was completed, an underlined theme surfaced that the leaders deemed their roles as one of a *"right of passage,"* a noble opportunity to serve the Senior Pastor and the church's congregants, and not one of secure status and privileged power. When deemed a privilege, leaders are more receptive to policies, procedures, and rules related to accountability and responsibility. Consequently, autocratic leadership creates a fear to move forward, anxiety to work together towards future purposes and a hostile environment in which to establish new leadership. In other words, tyrant leadership practices are against change and allergic to

---

[64] Ephesians 4:12 (New International Version)

accepting innovative notions that will help and not hinder the church's progress.[65]

Therefore, accountability and responsibility in my Leadership Development Program is defined as, *"holding self and others accountable for measurable high quality, timely and cost effective results while accepting responsibility for mistakes."*[66]   In this experience of establishing a paradigm of seeking and increasing new leadership in a timely matter, I discovered creating and developing a pipeline for new leadership is both a very daunting and challenging task to undertake; however, the end result or suggested outcome is not completely visible from the start. Often the steps necessary that lead to the desired outcome of developing and training leaders are mundane and not well received by others in the church during the creation process. As the leadership development curriculum was in its infancy, many senior leaders were unsure, hesitant, and somewhat resistant towards the concept for a new leadership program because they were comfortable and content with the previous model. As I started this initiative of rebuilding and rebranding our leadership, I was reminded of the Civil Rights trailblazer Frederick Douglass. He stated, *without struggle there will be no progress*[67]. Therefore, I took these initial challenges as a map to progress.

---

[65] Nate Booth, *Strategies for Fast-Changing Times,* (Rocklin: Prima, 1997), 151-155.

[66] Lovett H. Weems, Jr., *Church Leadership: Vision Team Cultural Integrity*, (Nashville: Abingdon Press, 2010), 15.

[67] Frederick Douglass, Goodreads-Quotable Quote, *Struggle and Progress,* http://www.goodreads.com/quotes/6398-if-there-is-no-struggle-there-is-no-progress-those=
(accessed March 4, 2014).

In the beginning stages of creating a viable Leadership Development Program, I realized the need to identify the weakness of the current leadership development efforts. The primary issue was there was no formal process to develop basic leadership skills on any level. More so, it was very inconsistent, confusing and a waste of time in seeking and developing new leaders. One of the prevailing weaknesses of leadership was the mindset of many senior leaders at the time. There was a false perception that leadership was about "position" and not about "action." Those leaders operated under the premise that leadership was limited to being served and not serving others. They wanted to be in the front of the line and did not seek to assist others in advancing to the front. They were authoritarians who only acknowledged the flaws and mistakes of the Senior Pastor; who discouraged change and governed legalistically by the policies and procedures of the church. I soon discovered in seeking change in the leadership structure that a down fall of this scheme of thought was that leaders only tell others "what to do" and "how to do," but they won't do.

As I developed a sustainable leadership development plan, there was no comprehensive definition of leadership or leader, other than an association with a title and power. Therefore, in my quest to equip, energize and empower new leadership in a timely manner, I established a clear, defined, and uniformed definition of *servant leadership*. In my description of a servant leader in my contextual setting, I closely relied on a standard definition of leadership instead of an established one for its transparency and for its practical implications. Therefore, the Grove's definition of a Servant Leader is one who takes responsibility for getting others to a predetermined destination through his/her ability to influence. Having a passion for God and God's people; possesses such noble characteristics as accountability, integrity, honesty, commitment, communication skills, and ability to follow while leading. One of the most important characteristics of a prospective leader, besides being considered a servant leader and faithfully supporting the Senior Pastor's vision and the church's mission, is for each to regularly contribute to the work of the ministry through their tithes and offerings. These spiritual attributes of a prospective leader at The Greater Piney Grove Baptist Church function in conjunction with what Jesus entrusted his disciples to lead from,"...*whoever wants to become great among you must be your servant, and whoever wants to be first must be slave of all.*"[68]

Creating and developing a leadership pipeline that will attract, equip, empower, and energize the targeted young adult group of prospective young vibrant leaders, I sought three areas of focus that must be thrust into the forefront for the success of this Leadership Development Plan. They are training leadership effectively, developing leaders efficiently, and empowering leaders successfully to lead and serve others. Training and development are essential to the continued growth and maturation of the church body. Initial training must be conducted for the leadership so they can be equipped to carry out the integral components of this plan. The conduit for this to take place is through the method of relationships, building secure and long last relationships between the Senior Pastor, the Senior Leadership team and potential leaders. Therefore, the first component of the Leadership Development plan is

---

[68] . Mark 10:43-44 (New International Version)

the training of the prospective leadership. This process includes ministry training and leadership accountability for the potential leader.

The Senior Leadership and I established the prospective leaders' Purpose Statements to become a Servant Leader at The Greater Piney Grove Baptist Church. They are as follows:

THE PURPOSE STATEMENTS OF BEING A PROSPECTIVE LEADER AT THE GREATER PINEY GROVE BAPTIST CHURCH

The Senior Leadership is to provide a systematic, yet responsive process for ongoing training and developing of the leadership of the church

The duty of potential leaders is to enhance the overall effectiveness of the program of the church, resulting in leadership development and spiritual growth.

To assure that our quest for excellence includes effective communication, development of relationships, spiritual connection and continual mentorship with Senior Leadership and Potential Leaders.

The Relationship Leadership Development

The Senior Leaders will meet together with the Prospective Leaders at least once a week. This meeting will include providing updates, guidance, direction, and reflections.

The Senior Leadership will provide the Prospective Leaders with the opportunity to observe ministry meetings, taking them with the Senior

Leadership on duty assignments (Outreach, Youth/Children's Church, Devotions, Road Team trips, and Servant Leader of the Week) and to also include them in ministry activities whenever possible and appropriate.

The Senior Leadership will attend each of the scheduled training sessions and any other activities with the Prospective Leader where their attendance as a body is requested.

The Senior Leadership should keep the Prospective Leader informed of all church and ministry activities.

The Spiritual Connection

The Senior Leadership and the Prospective Leader should always pray together at least once a week.

During the meditation and prayer time, the Senior Leadership should pray for the Prospective Leaders and their families to keep clear the works and service they are being considered to do and to continue to have a servant's heart.

The Senior Leadership and the Prospective Leader should always apply the divine disciplines of the church according to the Word of God as much as possible.

The Continual Mentorship

The Senior Leadership should allow for the Prospective Leader to be included on communion and hospital visits to sick, shut-in, and bereaved members and non-members.

The Senior Leadership should provide guidance, instructions, and wisdom on the roles and responsibilities of a Servant Leader constantly demonstrating and stressing the need for a servant work and heart.

The Senior Leadership should share with the Prospective Leader an exhaustive evaluation of their progress every three months of the training period.

The Senior Leadership will encourage the Prospective Leaders to be creative in their thinking to include seeking solutions to issues of the church, members, and non-members.

The Senior Leadership will always encourage and be supportive of the Prospective Leader by being an example to them in Christian conduct, support, and always be available to share with them ideas, experience, knowledge, and other help that maybe needed.

Next, we acquired General Goals and Strategies for those members seeking to become potential leaders and eventually becoming a Senior Servant at The Greater Piney Grove Baptist Church. They are as follows:

THE GENERAL GOALS & STRATEGIES OF PROSPECTIVE LEADERSHIP

The Senior Leadership Team developed goals and strategies to implement the plan. The Senior Leadership's responsibility during this time is to develop a leadership curriculum through classes for the ongoing effectiveness of the Grove's five-pillar ministry model: Teaching, Mission, Evangelism, Fellowship, and Worship. The Senior

Leader is to set forth the assignments, responsibilities, expectations, and requirements for potential leadership services at The Greater Piney Grove Baptist Church. Subsequently, this will be executed through three leadership development strategies. They are as follows:

Strategy 1:

Select and train potential persons who will be responsible for the leadership of each of the five pillars.

Each pillar will have three responsible leaders, as a result of the leadership training, who will become liaisons between the congregants, the Senior Leadership and the Senior Pastor.

Strategy 2:

The Senior Leadership will provide a process for regular and on-going spiritual growth for potential leaders through a 12 to 18 month course of training that includes workshops and hands-on experiences with a Senior Leader. This outcome is the establishment, as Lovett Weems suggest in structural leadership, "shared power" of ideas, notions and innovative impressions among the Senior Leadership and the Prospective Leader.[69]

The potential leader must be actively involved in church worship services, activities within and outside the church, and be aggressively enrolled in and regularly attend a Sunday school class and Bible Study.

---

[69] Lovett H. Weems, Jr. and Tom Berlin., *Bearing Fruit: Ministry with Real Results*, (Nashville: Abingdon Press, 2010), 37.

Potential Leaders must attend quarterly L.E.A.D.-*Leadership Empowerment And Development* sessions with The Senior Pastor.

Strategy 3:

Ensure that the quarterly L.E.A.D. sessions include specific components to aid leaders in conducting their activities in an excellent and responsible manner. This will include:

Various leadership training courses

Strategic planning training

Leadership responsibility and accountability

Leadership evaluation tools

Spiritual growth development for leaders

THE THREE PHRASES OF BEING A PROSPECTIVE LEADER TO BECOMING A SERVANT LEADER

"The Grove" needs to provide its prospective leaders, newly elected leaders, as well as its seasoned leaders with every opportunity to be nurtured and developed toward a life of servant leadership. Most of the development opportunities at "The Grove" are fellowship sessions disguised as development and training. The existence of a comprehensive leadership development plan will have a training curriculum with flexible modes of delivery while periodically assessing the effectiveness of existing leadership. This may cause two occurrences if executed correctly - relationship and shared power -

among both the Senior Leadership and Prospective Leaders.

3-Phases: *Leadership Development Plan*

To implement accurately, I am recommending a three phase training process for all prospective leaders. Existing leaders will only follow the last two phases of the process. Step one of the leadership development plan is *The Prerequisite Phase*, which consists of a personal and spiritual gifts questionnaire (See appendix #3). Step two of the leadership development plan is *The Preparation and Foundational Development Phase*. Lastly, one of the most important steps is *The Long Term Development Phase* through mentorship. Thusly, this pivotal phase will inspire leaders to move forward and be open to relevant changes and the future expansion of new leaders in a more dependable and timely matter. I estimate the overall implementation-to-conclusion calendar of the Leadership Development Plan will last approximately twelve to eighteen months.

Phase 1: *Prerequisite – Personal & Spiritual Assessment*

Phase one consists of a personal and spiritual assessment. The personal and spiritual assessment is for those individuals that may be asking themselves "do I have what it takes to be a servant leader at the Grove?" During this step, the prospective leaders, which are new candidates for leadership positions, will focus on "being a servant leader." During this step of the process, the candidates will be assessed on their Spiritual Gifts by using the attached assessment:

Phase one of the plan will last approximately one month. While the prospective leader is undergoing the spiritual gifts assessment, simultaneously the church body is conducting a nomination and recommendation for each prospective leader. The qualifications to nominate a prospective leader are as follows:

Must be member of the church for a minimum of 2 years

Extensive Background Check

Consistent Contributor (Tither) to the church

Consistent Steward of the day-to-day Operations of the church

Supporter of the Church's Mission and Vision

Loyal Advocate to the Senior Leadership and the Senior Pastor

After this initial process, the Senior Pastor will review, assesses, disapprove, or approve the nominated candidates. The candidates who advance will began the interview process as a potential leader. The potential leader will be interviewed by panel method consisting of the Leadership Executive Board Ministry. This 10 member panels consists of:

The Chairman of The Leadership Training

The Chairwoman of The Leadership Training

The Secretary of The Leadership Training

The Assistant Secretary of The Leadership Training

Four Senior Leaders

Two Appointed Lay Members

The interview questions are as follows:

1. Tell us about yourself, your education, background, profession, and family life?

2. What do you consider your most major accomplishment?

3. How is your spiritual life as it relates to relationship, spiritual covenant, and mentorship?

4. What are your interests in holding a leadership position at church?

5. What are your strengths, weaknesses and areas of improvement as a prospective leader (you can discuss within your profession, family life, community etc.)?

6. What are some skills you enjoy using as a potential leader?

7. Give an example of a challenge(s) or problem(s) you faced and how you dealt with it. Give another example.

8. As a potential leader, how would you improve the future outlook of The Greater Piney Grove Baptist Church?

9. Where do you feel you can contribute most at The Greater Piney Grove Baptist Church?

10. Which of the 5 pillars at The Greater Piney Grove Baptist Church do you currently serve in and in what capacity and what sparked your interest in the pillar?

Please note there is no particular order for the Executive Board Ministry to ask the interview questions to the aspiring candidate.

After interviews are completed, the Executive Ministry members will vote on each potential leader. Those who are voted successfully are then forwarded to the Senior Pastor for review, suggestions and final approval. Thereafter, both the Executive Ministry members and The Senior Pastor will present the recommendation of all the potential leaders who passed the prerequisite for the church body for official vote.

Phase 2: *Preparation – Foundational Development*

Phase two of the Leadership Development plan is preparation for becoming a leader through the fundamental and philosophical approach towards leadership, thusly named, *the Foundational Development*. This step is designed for the recently selected leader or those individuals that are thinking, now that I know what it takes to be a leader, what foundational skills do I need to learn to become a servant leader at The Grove. This individual should have passed through step one. This step is focused on becoming a servant leader at The Grove. During this step of the process, during the first month after becoming a leader, the candidates will develop an understanding that a call to lead is a call to prepare. The potential leader will understand servant leadership behaviors through the biblical concept of the following:

Spiritual Growth-Abide in Christ

Daily Growth-Live by God's Word

Faithful Growth-Pray in Faith

Relational Growth-Build Godly Relationships

Evangelic Growth-Witness to the World

Servant Growth- Minister to Others

Potential leaders will know The Grove's leadership expectations, which are as follows:

1. A commitment to growing a relationship with Jesus Christ

Attending regular Worship Service, Sunday Church School and regular Bible Study

2. A commitment to increasing knowledge of Jesus Christ through prayer and Study

3. A commitment to Stewardship & Sacrifice

4. A commitment to the Body of Christ at the Grove

Participation in Tribal Ministry, multiple service ministries, consistent participation in small groups, and celebration services and a commitment to increasing competency as a leader

Phase 3: *Practice – Long Term Development*

The final phase, and most significant, is the practice and continual mentorship through the long-term development of being an effective servant leader at The Greater Piney Grove Baptist Church. Phase three is the practice phase, which is long-term development. This phase is designed for all leaders at The Grove that have passed through steps one and two or seasoned leaders that did not go through the prerequisite and preparation steps that may be asking "what are the things I need to practice long-term to be effective as a leader at The Grove. This step is the longest phase lasting approximately 11 months. This step is focused on doing as a leader at The Grove. During this step of the process, generally after the first month or so after becoming a leader, the candidates will continually develop prescribed principles of servant leadership to include four Principles of Christian Leadership which are faithfulness, high standards, leading by example and inspiring cooperation from the heart.

Please note each Servant Leadership topic below takes approximately 2-3 class sessions to review, discuss, and complete. (See Appendix #4)

The Grove currently does not have an environmentally rich learning culture where our leaders are enthusiastic about learning for the sake of learning. As such, I recommend migrating from a single large group-learning format to a hybrid that includes large and small group learning formats. There will be quarterly conferences in large group format for Step 3 leaders. Those leaders in phases one and two will be supplemented with bi -monthly small group format. This includes Sunday Life School Class, which will train up to 15 leaders at a given session and the seven principles of Servant Leadership will also be taught at these sessions.

The seven principles of servant leadership are as follows:

1. Servant leaders humble themselves and wait for God to exalt them. (Luke 14:7-11)[70]

2. Servant leaders follow Jesus rather than positions. (Mark 10:32-40).[71]

3. Servant leaders give up personal rights to find greatness in service to others. (Mark 10:41-45)[72]

4. Servant leaders can risk serving others because they trust that God is in control of their lives. (John 13:3)[73]

5. Servant leaders take up Jesus' towel of servant hood to meet the needs of others. (John 13:4-11)[74]

6. Servant leaders share their responsibility and authority with others to meet a greater need. (Acts 6:1-6)[75]

7. Servant leaders multiply their leadership by empowering others to lead. (Exodus 18:17-23)[76]

The Learning Method will include in-class teams, cooperative note taking, and problem-based learning, think aloud pair problem solving, and scenario-based learning. The approaches to learning used will include:

---

[70] Luke 14:7-11 (King James Version)
[71] Mark 10:32-40 (King James Version)
[72] Mark 10:41-45 (King James Version)
[73] John 13:3 (King James Version)
[74] John 13:4-11 (King James Version)
[75] Acts 6:1-6 (King James Version)
[76] Exodus 18:17-23 (King James Version)

- Verbal- The Lessons of King Solomon

- Logical- The Concept and Teaching of Paul

- Visual-The Understanding of John and his Revelation

- Physical-The Study of the Prophet Ezekiel

- Musical-The Study of The Psalmist David

- Natural-The Principle of King David

- Relational-Life Lesson from the Relationship Between Barnabas and Saul (Paul)

For those leaders who are in phases one and two, the learning sessions will take place during Sunday Life School hours. Leadership development training will occur every other month during the regularly scheduled Sunday Church School hours, which are held each Sunday either at 7:30 am or 9:30 am. For leaders who are in phase three, the learning sessions will take place during quarterly conference meeting with Senior Pastor immediately following Bible Study. Sessions for those in phrases one and two will last approximately 90 to 120 minutes. The sessions for phase three leaders will last approximately 45 minutes to 60 minutes. Again, the curriculum may take up to 12 to 18 months to complete. Subsequently, once we get a critical mass of ministry leaders through Step 3, we can then implement a "Train-the-Trainer" approach to sustain a learning atmosphere, which the Prospective Leaders will have the opportunity to teach or train the Senior Leaders. This action will cause the Senior Leader and the Prospective leader to train each other through the avenue of relationship building, spiritual covenant, and continual mentorship. Accordingly, this necessary method between Senior Leadership and Prospective Leader will produce a cohesive ambience of being energized, equipped, and empowered to not only be an influential servant leader, but also motivated to serve others. As a result of successfully going through the structured leadership development program at The Grove, it is our expectation that the learners will be equipped with the following learning outcomes:

Learning Outcomes:

- Understand the spiritual gifts given to them by God

- Identify servant leadership skills and behaviours

- Assess one's own spiritual growth, approach to learning, and communications style

- Understand The Grove's expectation of its servant leaders

- Lead and serve like Jesus in their daily walk and relationships

- Communicate effectively with other leaders and followers using verbal and non-verbal communications skills

- Successfully recruit other servant volunteers

- Build effective teams of servant volunteers

- Resolve conflicts using various techniques

- Apply numerous laws and life changing principles of irrefutable leadership to everyday life

- Understand Christ's strategy of Evangelism through biblical principles

- Understand how "effective ministry" fosters significant and continual changes in how people live

- Become a successful vertical servant leader (see things from God's perspective and help others discover what they were created to do)

THE EVALUATION, THE PRESBYTERY AND ORDINATION

Finally, after the prospective leader has completed the three phases of The Greater Piney Grove Baptist Church's leadership plan, the Senior Leader who sponsored a prospective leader does an extensive evaluation of the candidate. To name a few, the evaluation of the candidate includes the following,

Did the prospective leader fulfil all requirements to be considered a Servant Leader?

Did the prospective leader actively attend, participate, and complete all course work?

Does the prospective leader have the characteristics, the spiritual components and demeanour of a Servant Leader who abides in Christ, live by HIS word, who indeed is a consistent steward of the church and most importantly is loyal to the Senior Pastor to carry out, on his behalf, the church's vision and mission?

Does the prospective leader fully understand the principles,

93

mannerisms and biblical components of Servant Leadership?

Does the prospective leader display a commitment to growing in Jesus Christ through prayer and Study as a Servant Leader after this process is completed?

Following the extensive evaluation of the prospective leader, and if they meet all requirements, their name is recommended to the Senior Pastor and the Senior Leadership Ministry for Presbytery and Ordination Service.

Interestingly, some may ask does the Baptist church indeed have its own principles and guidelines pertaining to ordaining servant leaders within the Baptist tradition? The distinction of the Baptist paradigm from other denominations is the Baptist church believes every church is autonomous.   Meaning each Baptist church selects its own pastor, servant leaders, governs its own church, and each determines their own policies and procedures without outside control or supervision. Therefore, each Baptist church is unique based on its pastor, leadership, tradition, culture and the surrounding community. The Greater Piney Grove Baptist Church prefers to follow the Presbyterian format of ordaining servant leaders. Similar to the Presbytery doctrine, we too believe the scriptural implication of ordination is for one to be set aside, consecrated, ordained, conferred and appointed by God in Christian servanthood through one's ministerial gift.[77] Likewise, Christ ordained the twelve, whom he earlier claimed as his disciples but later named the Apostles who ultimately established His kingdom. In conjunction with

---

[77] T. DeWitt Smith, Jr., *The New Testament Deacon Ministry in African American Churches,* (Atlanta: Hope House, 1994), 11-15.

these scriptural principles, my church ordains prospective leaders as Christ ordained his disciples to serve HIS people.[78] Therefore, these are the guidelines developed by the Senior Leadership for Presbytery and Ordination Service:

- The Preliminary Preparations of Presbytery

- Prospective Leaders who are to be ordained as Servant Leaders are those who have been officially voted by the church body.

- The Senior Pastor has spent a considerable amount of time with Prospective Leader.

- Be ready to inform Presbytery of any request by the prospective Candidate, Church, or Pastor.

- Thirty minutes prior to start of Presbytery, each candidate will meet with the Senior Pastor, Chairs of Servant Leaders Ministry, and Senior Leadership Ministry.

- The Senior Pastor/Chairman of Servant Leaders Ministry will provide instructions to Presbytery members on the order of the Presbytery.

- Begin and close with prayer.

---

[78] Matthew 28:16-20 (NKJV)

The Day of Presbytery (usually the day before Ordination Service)

1. The Senior Pastor presides over Presbytery Council.

2. The Senior Pastor serves as temporary moderator of Presbytery until a moderator is elected.

Elect the following:

- Moderator of the presbytery.

- Clerk of the presbytery.

- Instructions will be provided to the presbytery as to

- Designated questions for prospective candidate or candidates

- Number of questions asked of prospective candidate

- How many prospective candidates will be questioned at any given time

- Who can ask questions of the prospective candidate

- Next, Presbytery Council Moderator calls for the spokesman of the church to present the prospective candidate to the presbytery.

- The Presbytery Council Moderator calls for the person who is to question the candidates to begin the examination

- After examination is finished, the Moderator calls for a motion and second to recommend or not to recommend those who are being considered by the church for ordination

The Order of Ordination Service (the following day)

After each potential candidate has gone through the Presbytery Council, been examined and questioned; the prospective candidate is invited to the ordination service or ceremony to officially commence Servant Leadership in The Greater Piney Grove Baptist Church. This is officially carried out during the following Sunday evening service. Below is a template of the order of an ordination service:

The Prelude

The Call to Worship

The Processional of The Senior Pastor, The First Lady, Guest Ministers, and Prospective Leaders

The Welcome

The Reading of Scripture

The Congregational Prayer

The Choral Selection

The Offertory Period

The Introduction of Preacher

The Song of Sermonic Preparation

The Ordination Sermon

(Normally given by a guest minister who the Senior Pastor has extended an invitation)

The Invitation to Discipleship

The Ordination and Consecration of Prospective Leaders Ceremony begins

The Statement of Purpose

The Senior Pastor calls for the reading of the minutes of the organization of the Presbytery Council

The Report of the Presbytery Council

The clerk of Presbytery Council reads minutes of the organization of the Presbytery, examination of candidates, and recommendations of Presbytery

The Statement of Affirmation to the Prospective Leaders

The Senior Pastor calls for the recommendations of the Prospective Leaders to be presented to the church for approval as servant leaders of the church. When it is approved by the congregation the service continues.

The Charge to the Prospective Leaders

The Ordination Prayer and The Laying of Hands

Special Presentation and Award of servant leader certificate of license to each Prospective Leader

Benediction and Blessing

Chapter 4.

THE CONCLUSION:

Where Do We Go From Here: Building Unity Amidst Diversity As We Become Servant Leaders?

No one puts new wine into old wineskins; or else the new wine will burst the wineskins and be spilled, and the wineskins will be ruined.[79]

-Jesus, The Christ

I believe in any leadership role and whenever one completes a task, whether it is rewarding or overwhelming, one should always be willing to reflect, evaluate, and ask the imperative question, *where do we go from here?* Likewise, I too, must ask myself after this vast experience of The Greater Piney Grove Baptist Church's traditional dynamic that now empowers transformational leadership. Indeed, where does The Greater Piney Grove Baptist Church go from here as we continue to strive to build unity amidst a diverse church and society to energize, equip, and empower others to become servant leaders?

As I reflect upon this experience after studying carefully the rich history, culture change, dynamics and shifts *The Grove has undergone*, and chronicling the journey of our newly ordained Senior leaders, it is evident that if The Greater Piney Grove Baptist Church will continue to thrive it must continue the legacy and rich heritage of an ever-evolving church ministry by being poised to move without hesitation, with a

---

[79] Luke 5:37 (NKJV)

humble heart and holy boldness to the next level in ministry. To further survive in the 21st century in an ever-changing church and beyond, The Greater Piney Grove Baptist Church must deliberately train and continue to develop new leaders in a timely manner to undertake trends many traditional black Baptist churches do not readily embrace. Thereby, in order for The Greater Piney Grove Baptist Church's leadership paradigm to serve the present age, redeem lost souls and revive lost passion in her leaders, the current senior leaders must freely embrace shifts in our church dynamics and a transformational leadership structure that is inclusive and not exclusive to a particular gender, status, and age.

In creating a ministry of excellence through The Greater Piney Baptist Church's leadership prototype that will glorify the Father, exalt and manifest our Christ, as well as edify the body, we must critically assess the shifts and changes that are inevitable in church growth and development.

WHAT DID I LEARN WHILE IMPLEMENTING LEADERSHIP CHANGE

In setting forward in my charge to change the traditional dynamic through transformational leadership, while easing the anxiety of senior members, I had to stay consistent and focused through this life-changing experience. I deliberately worked hard in balancing the shared assumptions of the more seasoned members of *The Grove* with those of the progressive young adults and youth members who found our church culture attractive. I desired to meet the needs of those in the newly flourishing and progressive church, while also tending to those members who were still adapting to the transition in the mission, focus and goals.

In my role as Executive Pastor, with the permission from the Senior Pastor, I sought to continue to lead our church forward in maturity and embrace with confidence the promises of the future. In response to leadership readiness, I wanted to continue to enhance the church's relevance through various resources to reach the least, the lost, and forgotten. In other words, through this experience I aspired to set the standard for our church to always be moving progressively forward while producing future leaders who are forward thinkers and not past dwellers.

In doing so, I am more mindful to constantly assess the dynamics of our church and the culture that's birthed from our church as it relates to our members and the surrounding community. It is my yearning to always be a church that produces and reproduces potential leaders who are innovative thinkers who lead despite culture change and without anxiety. In staying current with the needs of the 21st century church, I will continue to survey the prospective needs of our congregants so we will be able to develop leaders who are proactive, rather than reactive in breaking down the barriers of tradition. I believe with this newly established development plan and leadership curriculum, The Greater Piney Baptist Church and I are both successfully moving in the right direction.

Moreover, in serving my church as an effective leader, I seek to continue to work closely with the Senior Pastor and leadership team ministry to discuss the latest trends, to assess the current shifts, and

103

evaluate those dynamics of the church that may hinder us from moving onward as we develop more leaders. As a leader, I learned to be objective so that I can always be fresh in operation. Thereby, I can lead in hopes that I can be honest, and perceptive to indicators of division early on, while being equipped to empower new leaders to identify the problems and the solutions.

In closing this leadership assessment of The Greater Piney Grove Baptist Church, I am proud to be a part of a church structure that invests in leadership. My focus and determination now is progressive and spirit-driven. In watching our church transform in the past twenty-four years, I am forging ahead to continue the momentum of educating and maintaining effective leadership.

Additionally, I understand now how the traditional members who were from a different class and age bracket felt when a different culture was introduced, and why they did not initially embrace new leadership and creativity view in a timely manner. Throughout this process, I recognized the parable of Jesus holds truth when bringing to traditional values when he advises, *no one puts new wine into old wineskins; or else the new wine will burst the wineskins and be spilled, and the wineskins will be ruined.*[80] It is evident that a leader can't produce fresh and innovative from something that is already established and conventional because as the parable implies the tradition will be ruined, and the resentment caused will hinder any prospects for progress. Nevertheless, the parable of Jesus guided me in distinguishing between the old and the new, the traditions of a church, and how to effectively

---

[80] Luke 5:37 (NKJV)

institute or implement change without ruining the tradition, yet enhancing it.

 In the beginning, due to my impatience I was not careful enough to examine the layers; and the significance of culture and tradition that confronted my vision of progress when I sought to train new leaders. In setting my roadmap, I began to analyze the difference in culture that the new leadership and surrounding community reflected. I acknowledged in undergoing several phases in the lifecycle of The Greater Piney Grove Baptist Church that in order to incorporate new leadership in a traditional dynamic, I first had to accept the existing leaders with their blend of values and norms. As result of the diverse brand of new leadership that reflects new subcultures, my church is now more open, honest, positive and attracted to potent ideas that will sustain us as we embark on future challenges and changes. To lessen the divides within a congregation, I learned it is necessary to acknowledge the large effect of culture within it.

After analyzing the challenges faced throughout the various phases that our church experienced, I am better positioned to lead our congregation forward successfully without returning to the traditional model of leadership. As a core leader at my church, who is connected to the large and dominate subculture of young adults, I will continue to push technology to train new leaders, while bringing the more traditional subculture along in keeping abreast of the changes taking place to keep our church moving forward.

In the roadmap for continued growth our focus on 21st century technology is to also embrace and engage the youth in worship. By investing in our future (church), we are deliberately keeping our vision fresh and in action. As a church that plans to continue its success in the years to come, we must focus on the dynamics of each subculture as we service the needs of them collectively.

If the church is to be the refuge in the 21st century and beyond, we must develop current and future leaders who will be trained to take the church to the next dimension where the disenfranchised can be redeemed, reconciled, restored, and revived, and welcomed into a right relationship with God and full fellowship with Christ and His people.

Ultimately, my vision is to continue to create unity through the pathway of servant leadership on the cornerstone of our mission and vision in building a legacy of effective, influential leaders in a church that lives up to her name, The *"Greater"* Piney Grove Baptist Church.

FLIPPIN LEGACY MINISTRIES

With the release of my book, I would like to offer my consultative services to facilitate and conduct a workshop at your church for either prospective leaders or young adults, ages 18-40 on how to reach and more importantly sustain young adults. For allowing me to conduct a workshop, an honorarium is not a requirement; although it would be welcomed. The only request I have when I facilitate is to be allowed to sale my new book and workbook to all those who attend and would like to purchase it.

If you are interested, please feel free to contact me anytime via email, RevRCFlip@aol.com or by way of my cell phone: 770-289-7952. Thank you for your sincere consideration.

Kind Regards,

Rev. Dr. Richard C. Flippin

BIBLIOGRAPHY

Agosto, Efrain. *Servant Leadership: Jesus & Paul*. St. Louis: Chalice Press, 2005.

Baldwin, James. Goodreads- Quotable Quote, *Knowing*

http://www.goodreads.com/quotes/14373-know-from-whence-you-came-if-you-know-whence-you. (accessed March 13, 2014).

Blanchard, Ken and Phil Hodges. *Lead Like Jesus: Lesson from The Greatest Role Model of All Time,* Nashville: Thomas Nelson, 2005.

Booth, Nate. *Strategies for Fast-Changing Times.* Rocklin: Prima, 1997.

Boulding, Kenneth. *"Concept of Leadership,"* http://www.nwlink.com/~donclark/leader/leadcon.html (accessed October 20, 2013).

Chand, Samuel R. *Cracking Your Church's Culture Code: Seven Keys to Unleashing Vision & Inspiration.* San Francisco: Jossey-Bass, 2011.

Chand, Samuel R. *What's Shakin' Your Ladder?* Niles, IL: Mall Publishing, 2005.

Chand, Samuel R. *Who's Holding Your Ladder?* Niles, IL: Mall Publishing, 2003.

Gandhi, Mahatma. Brainy Quotes, *Servanthood,* http://www.brainyquote.com/quotes/quotes/m/mahatmagan150725.html. (accessed March 13, 2014).

Greenleaf, Robert K. *"The Concept of Servant Leadership"* 16 (May 2002): 27, http://www.regent.edu/acad/global/publications/jvl/vol1_iss1/Spears_Final.pdf (accessed October 20, 2013).

Greenleaf, Robert. S*ervant Leadership Quotes Put Others First,* http://www.youreffectiveleadership.com/servant-leadership-quotes.html (accessed March 13, 2014).

King, Jr., Martin Luther, Clayborne Carson (Editor), Ralph E. Luker (Editor) and Denny A. Russell (Editor). *The Papers of Martin Luther King, Jr.: Volume 1: Called to Serve, January, 1929-June, 1951.* Martin Luther King Papers [Hardcopy]. California: University of California, 1992.

Larson, Craig Brain. 750 Engaging Illustrations for Preachers, Teachers and Writers, Grand Rapids: Barker Books, 2007.

Maxwell, John C. Maxwell. *Developing The Leader Within You,* Nashville: Thomas Nelson, 1993.

Maxwell, John C. Maxwell. *The 21 Irrefutable Laws of Leadership,* Nashville: Thomas Nelson, 1998.

Maxwell, John C. Maxwell. *The 360-Degree Leader,* Nashville, TN: Thomas Nelson, 2005.

McCarthy, Jim. "Change Management versus Transition Management." Article, 1 (June, 2011) http://www.jimmccarthyonline.com/2009/06/123/.

Riley, Pat. *The Winner Within,* New York: Berkley Publishing, 1994.

Roozen, David A. Faith Communities Today Article. *A Decade of Change in American Congregations,* 25 (June 2010): www.faithcommunitiestoday.org. (accessed November 13, 2013).

Schein, Edgar H. Schein. *Organizational Culture and Leadership*, 3rd Edition, San Francisco: Jossey-Bass, 2004; a Wiley imprint.

Smith, T. DeWitt., Jr. *The New Testament Deacon Ministry in African American Churches,* Atlanta: Hope House, 1994.

Thompson, George B., Jr. *How to Get Along With Your Pastor: Creating Partnership for Doing Ministry*, Cleveland: Pilgrim Press, 2006.

Thompson, George B., Jr. *Treasure in Clay Jars: New Ways to Understand Your Church*, Cleveland: Pilgrim Press, 2003.

Weems, Lovett H., Jr. and Tom Berlin. *Bearing Fruit: Ministry with Real Results*, Nashville: Abingdon Press, 2010.

Weems, Lovett H., Jr. *Church Leadership: Vision Team Cultural Integrity,* Nashville: Abingdon Press, 2010.

Made in the USA
Charleston, SC
18 October 2016